Even The
Java
Sparrows
Call
Your
Hair

Also by George Kalamaras

Poetry
Borders My Bent Toward (2003)
The Theory and Function of Mangoes (2000)

Poetry Chapbooks
Beneath the Breath (1988)
Heart Without End (1986)

Criticism
Reclaiming the Tacit Dimension:
Symbolic Form in the Rhetoric of Silence (1994)

Even The Java Sparrows Call Your Hair

George
Kalamaras

Quale Press

AUTHOR'S NOTE: I want to extend my deep thanks to my parents, family, teachers, and friends for supporting my writing over the years, and to Gian Lombardo and Quale Press for taking this project on and for a terrific job in all its phases. I offer very special thanks to my compadres—those great troubadours of the prose poem—Eric Baus, John Bradley, Ray Gonzalez, Jim Grabill, Patrick Lawler, Paul Roth, and John Yau for their friendship, love, support, and brotherhood in the work, and to Eric Baus, John Bradley, Forrest Gander, Jim Grabill, and Judy Johnson for their abundant conversation and commentary about this book. Immeasurable gratitude to my wife, Mary Ann Cain, for being "the one" in all things we so sweetly share—meditation, writing, and love.

Acknowledgments continue on page 108.

Cover: "The Call of the Night" by Paul Delvaux (oil on canvas, 113 x 133 cm, 1937, private collection), © 2004 Artists Rights Society (ARS), New York/SABAM, Brussels.

ISBN: 0-9744503-2-4 trade paperback edition

LCCN: 2004111727

Quale Press
www.quale.com

CONTENTS

for Mary Ann, always

and for the beloved yogis of India

Sparrows and sparrows;
no one's voice—how lovely—
stands out.

    —Yannis Ritsos, *3 x 111 Tristichs*

LONG YEARS
OF THE THROAT

IN THE CAFÉ OF STRANGE SKIN

In the café of strange skin, some woman or other was always staring vacantly into me as if she belonged to Delvaux. I had been a curator, that lifetime, in New Delhi, just back from a book-buying expedition in Lisbon. When I opened the moon, the train platform roared as if surrounded in birds, as if I was no longer alive, bitten by bees, and returned to my sorrowful bed of straw. It was a situation unlike no other, and I did not want to repeat it, even though I craved Greek pastry, *galaktaboureko* or *halvah*. In the café of strange skin, I was under the cruel influence of coffee. I had been star-bitten, hard, and required anything remotely bitter to calm me down. Absorbed in raking gravel through the chest cavity of a crow, I was beside myself with a contact of small friends. Even the squirrel knew my name in Maharashtran meant *school of established mustaches*. I required a requiem, requisite medicines found only in the bone-worship practiced by seasoned elephants. I needed the ancestor's tired tusk passed trunk to trunk among the herd, sniffed—after a year of death and great migration—for the proper flea scent and yeast. I opened the bite bitten into me by bees, in the café of strange skin. I wondered why they bit and did not sting, why each lamp-bearing nude reclining in the almost-pleasure moan of every conceivable position belonged only to me.

YOUR INSIDES HAVE
SOME EXPLAINING TO DO

Now we come to the study of blind ravens. We expiate the Gobi, we retract even the Punjab's coals. I wear a black cape and conjugate burnt particles of popcorn. I keep coming up with the number one, no matter how many times I count my toes. It seemed necessary to sleep with the eye open. Even if it meant wearing a mask, I could somehow see more deeply into the blind depths of my past. I could run guns, again, to Shoa with Rimbaud. When the fire ants from Namibia arrived, they were more than a memory. I knew they had invisibly implanted themselves below the skin and could be traced to my vigorous eczema. Psoriasis of the scrotum? Fierce bouts of almost-kissing? Inflammation of the preterit as one way to measure the jungle girth of my mouth? Decrepit blind Java sparrow as indicative of how to hop again on one foot, even as an adult? You're fed up, you tell me, that I keep inscribing my name throughout the tough wall of your intestinal tract. You believe I have eaten the poisonous plant, and—in eating me—you've invested the blind camel. Let me assuage any childhurt, let me assure. I've never been inside you the way two people were meant to bleed. My lapwing sting might be thrown as bones for dice. I am comfortably afar, counting my toes—cold-blooded—up to the number one. That writing inside you may or may not be sparrow, be blind, become, is more like bird track, I hear, or frustrated fists of ordinary cabbage railing to get out.

BRAHMS AND
THE TAXIDERMIES OF SLEEP

She dreamed I had died, head-wound fate of a flight of stairs. When I woke, my leg was cramped, my breath uneasy and short. She had dreamed me into a café, sipping tea with Brahms, interrogating him about the violin that became a blind owlet in the third movement of the third symphony. He had suggested Russian tea with rosehips and cloves. I had argued the merits of curing a cello with salt.

I was scared enough to light a candle upon waking, she confided. I felt it singe some dark smear into my cheek when she bent her loose nightclothes over me, inspecting my skull, quietly fingering it so as not to wake me. *What really disturbed me,* she later admitted, *wasn't the snail curve of owl blood on the pillow, but the gills you had grown, how the candle made them fade. That, and Brahms, of course,* she continued. *At least until both he and that baton dissolved when I tilted hot wax into your left ear, saying,* SHOO! GO HOME! LEAVE US BOTH ALONE!

So You Do

A woman hands you a hibiscus flower reddened with rain. You've seen her before, but the field mice at your feet don't look familiar. You sniff it and your throat tightens and your eyes go white. You feel as if you could swallow through your ears. You lie in a marsh on top of an eel spine, breathing through your feet. But you are dry and indoors. Someone has placed your hands together on your chest in prayer, and you wish they hadn't dressed you in that blue Hawaiian shirt.

Just then Julius Caesar walks into the parlor and begins making Turkish coffee. You want some, but the stiffness in your joints prevents you from getting up. An old girlfriend brings in donuts and rolls. She is naked except for a blue denim skirt and a gold necklace at her throat, and when she leans over you a tear oozes from her left nipple.

The Greek Orthodox priest is playing a Bengali harmonium and singing Hindu chants. His hair is long and matted, and his body is smeared with cremation ash from the Ganges. Your parents couldn't come because of the airfare from Florida. Your wife sits in white, beneath a NO SMOKING sign, drawing on a Camel, though she has never smoked, and eases her left foot in and out, in and out of her Bierkenstocks. Someone brings in a honey-baked ham, genuflects, and leaves.

The woman is busy arranging laundry baskets in the corner beneath pink lights. *One one-thousand, two one-thousand,* she begins, scratching her head, then her arm pits, with an orange-red stem. *Maybe I should get up and help,* you think, counting on your fingers her breathing up to ten. So you do, and they all greet you as if you'd just returned from the war. Uncle Ted wants to know if you'd like a Pepsi. The Jones' golden retriever brings you a dead bird. Four-year-old Henry from across the street asks you to bat a balloon in a game he invents called *Keep It Up in the Air*. Your brother Perry hands you a CD containing Jimi Hendrix's "1983 . . . (A Merman I Should Turn to Be)." Then your wife hugs you, says she loves you, that she didn't mean to smoke, that it was just for the taste and only because you had seemed so distant lately. Then she asks you to go home, remove the summer screens on the porch, replace the storms. Caesar puts his left arm around your shoulders, saying something about *my boy* and *the price of stocks* and *those damn cracks in the aqueducts resembling heat lightning in Carthage*. You promise to help him mortar them the next time you're in town.

THEY BROUGHT THE STONE

They brought the stone containing my birth date and a woman's left breast. I kissed it, clutched my navel, called it *Stavroula*, called it *OM*, referred to it as *best bird's beak in my chest*. I pictured my grandmother from Solake when she was old and could barely remember my name, asking if it was *candle* or *crayon* or *less than or equal to*. The stone was cold, hobbled my lower lip with a hexagon of hired hieroglyphics, constrained roses and uncompleted hyphens and the mournful scroll of *beloved whooping cough* and *devoted devotee of fly-squat and cranes*.

Someone told me my icon had begun to weep sandalwood paste. Saint George covered in the cremation ash of a Ganges River sadhu. Something was trying to live or die. Some tanager throng in my chest. Over and over. They beat its wings with a broom. They beat its wing, calling me *traitor, turncoat,* even saying I was speckled, brown, and blind, that my name had never been *Giorgos* after all, but *starling* or *sparrow stew* or *soggy Indiana ground,* perhaps only the revolving wind whoosh of *oo* and *ah*.

The stone was the exact weight and sphex of my lip, minus (of course) the thunder. I knew I could use it to startle the town into lightning, to chew jagged milk from a goat, to soak the hind leg of a fly into a hexagon of great good fortune. I cursed its scrawl and subsequent scratch, gripped its birth-date bliss with every Sanskrit grain that graveled my chest, with each blessing born from the rake and screw and almost-sound uttered from the thorax-fix, lodged at length—but released at last—from the smiles and fibrillations, from the cat-nap scratch of waking sleep and long years of the throat.

FROM
THE BOOK OF TONGUES (3)

dear epinastic urge,

There is a star in my throat. Some say *taxidermy*. But that's in my chest. It was my grandfather's pheasant. My grandmother who left her wheel mark in my thigh. Which is one season I've sunk backwards toward the ground of a dying star. Sometimes I wish I *could* die like a scar that can never quite heal. That piece of glass, the pavement crack, and, oh, how the tricycle never bleeds.

You crawled out to me last night, scrawled *pheasant* into my lowest bone. I am sorry to have startled you so. Who would have thought handing someone this *Book of Tongues* would create such a heat. For some time I thought the star was dying in *you*, felt its procreative pulse. Even got hard. Thirsty as salt. And weepy. At least when I stood naked and wanted nothing more than to clutch the gravity of plants.

You say I may secretly be a hosta. Perhaps a forsythia. But I beg you to return the salt tablets so that I may inscribe my host into the rain that is sure to return next week. That's one season I've cried to write my name backwards, three times with my head turned to the left, weeping into my own palm. No, I am not concerned that the bee entrail will expose your other (less convincing) urge. Who would have thought even bringing that up would have sent you pasting pictures of eels into every *Book of Tongues* you could locate. Which is one reason snail sliver enlivens my sheets. Even when not wet with the imagined tongue of her mouth.

Write when you survive. I know you are near, nestled against my frenum. Still, the spur in my ear is making your voice ease out of the plants, making me deaf with the unheard waves of eelgrass in wind. With knocks of knotty pine. With the pheasant tail pointing toward me forty years from the rec-room wall. I will, of course, respond. But I cannot be held responsible if you become a peacock again in a future life, and me an eel. Oh God, why a *wheel*? To have to be fourteen again and spilled with contusions? Sometimes I wish I could die—*when* I die—like a scar on glass against the risen sun.

WILLIAMS IN THE HOSPITAL, 1952

based on a photograph by Alfred Eisenstaedt

I found it in a rare book, water-marked and stained, that photograph of William Carlos Williams and an infant looking back at the good doctor, blurry-eyed and weeping. Williams' left hand consolingly on its right elbow, his mouth open as if to say *Googly-goo. Now what's wrong with you?* This profile of Williams' dark furry brow arched above glasses that study the multiple causes of pain. The beginning of the world and its untimely end. The infant stares back, mouth held in horror at the good doctor's touch, a perpetual wail wrangling from its prune-faced scowl. Its tiny ribs exposed like the breathing flank of a young zebra, stunned and panting fifty years through the black and white film. The sternum expanded and strained from the strength of so much weeping. Is it a little boy- or little girl-scream I see, forcing its frown forever into Williams' brow? Bare-chested wrangler who might one day grow up to herd cattle, dance ballet, hoist iron from a 13th floor scaffold. Who might one day bend to tenderly kiss a child of its own, try to calm it from some other terrible blight. Williams keeps leaning toward it, toward me, with fatherly concern, his white coat bunched at the collar, the knot in his necktie a way to make visible that knot hidden in his throat. His stethoscope sways like an unattached organ. He keeps holding the arm of the tiny child like the handle of a moving mirror. He steadies himself in the study, hears his first name perpetually echoed in his last. *It's okay, googly-goo,* he says. *Who are you?*

THE SANCTITY

And if they go to shoot you, remember, keep your mouth shut,
breathed the old man, leaning over him. *And careful to
always wear your thickest shirt, or the heat from your belly
will rush out all at once and leave you empty.*

But Lefteris wasn't listening again. He sat at the bar,
deep in some other music—the amber stirring of his
whiskey, the secrets of the glass only the coldness of the
ice knew—watching across the smoke a woman watch-
ing *him,* stroking with her hands the lull of her breasts.

The moon's sigh poured across the bar, spilling its sack
of flour. Through the window he could see snow piling
up, that little sound or drift of vowel whose cart could
carry him.

From the distance, a familiar breathing, a moist trem-
bling arose, close, as if from his own skin, like a life he
could not prove, like the scent of his mother's voice he
carried, still.

Tonight, he thought, in the flesh of some absolute
sound, he could die, perfectly.

dear bemoaned swan seed,

I slip through my teeth, come apart sucking my moan.

A piano quartet dissolves a vowel. Down through my spine.

Grounds too mulch to be seed. Footfall I might if I could.

I have eaten my entwined kind of night after night. Star. Of starlight. Starfish sewn into the left-infested coffee stain on my vest.

One mouth. Two. Three at a *the*. At an *a,* or *ah,* or *uh*.

Oh, the pranic seed is accelerating. My most wanted. Van Gogh's lost left sock. Delvaux's entire tongue. Brahms. Earwig. I turn blur the third ring of Saturn. Grid of my growth. Times three times thirteen.

A piano sextet. Five-pointed starfish pulse one expiring seed. Slow consonance of eel-fire lift. I slip into. Through. Come up. Soaking. Feather blear. Stain in the groan white. In the still pond sift. Of perfect. Soma. Sulch. Ornithologic. Tongue turned back upon its shelf of milk.

SOMA: IT IS RAINING

Waves of tortoise hair pour down, the way women's voices enter us as they touch each other open in separate rooms.

~

Mist lifts from the long rain of a rock the corpse exhales into its fragrant grass sprouting near his moist nipple.

~

What we move toward in the long grass is what we once were held by. Root of moonlight. Centipede in dusk.

~

The sky storms down like the insomniac's color he descends toward through the burning stairwell in his cigarette.

~

The dark wood of the knife respects the slice of onion, alone on its wooden board. *It is not easy,* the knife thinks, *being an onion.*

~

An onion of sleep drifts near the scent of lovers, alone in separate cities, lying still in blossoming milk their soil leaves.

~

What a man sees through a woman's dream darkens what he hears through.

~

A young girl's voice opens, like something final, a huge hope in a drop of milk.

THE EGG

Let's just call it an egg. It was something like an egg laid by a young woman.
— Kasuya Eiichi

What did her mother say, staring down at the brown thing which, when dry, fell oval into the rain-soaked Miyuki night like water seeking its own level? *My daughter must secretly be an ostrich. Either that or she's been French kissing the backyard birds again rather than feeding them bread.*

What did the midwife say, careful not to crack it open once it dropped—the young woman screaming one final push, clutching, on her cot, the metal rake? *Good girl! There! You've given birth to a—well, actually, you just laid a beautiful, healthy, seven-pound egg.*

What did the doctor say, descending onto the running board, turning at midnight to the coachman they had sent to the city to help with this emergency? *I hear the world is now oval, and all seven oceans contain speckled brown ostrich sperm. We need different colored paint for the scholastic globes! And from now on, every woman will have to be careful where she swims.*

What did the young father say, slumped on a stump at the local tavern, his buddies ribbing him with the news just brought by Koto, the fisherboy? *I don't give a damn. I'm only seventeen and I'm not getting married. Anyway, maybe it's really a carp and not an ostrich. Maybe it'll die if she doesn't hatch it in a warm tub or in some Shinto temple pool.*

What did the moon say, bending down through willows and the bare window into it, broadening it with that languid liquid gaze into a three-dimensional watery monocle? (No one heard what the moon said exactly, but there are accounts of clouds quickly converging to cover it, and the wind suddenly stopping, then violently moaning as if sucking back into itself.)

What did the mother say, lying there in the hut on a straw cot, having clutched the rake with sweating palms, having bathed the egg with bright blood-light, having watched the midwife lift it into the glow of the flickering lantern, gasp, spank it gently, and then clean it, having gotten it back, holding it in a blanket in her arms like a delicate cabbage head, encouraging it to her breast? *You're perfect. You're so perfect. You must now try to find a way to feed, my little darling, for the long journey ahead.* And then spreading her legs, pleading with the midwife, *Oh Madame, please, don't stop. Keep looking. Maybe there's an umbilical cord in there yet, a floating fluid crowbar, afraid to come out.*

I MIGHT AND SHE MIGHT

And so I struggled with wanting the width of her hips. She was as voluptuous as the woman seated alone, cupping her bare breasts, in Delvaux's *The Visit*. But I was no longer the surprised ten-year-old boy walking naked into her room. My testes had dropped, making me feel the full gravity of my blood flow. In those days, nipple piercing was not an option. Nor was completely shaving the amber beads from her underarms. I wanted the shade of that room, exactly as she dreamed it in moistening toward me her lip. I wanted her hips, proud and full as an unsucked plum. I could become an architect and fail to dissolve the fourth and fifth rings of Saturn. I knew my life depended on it. To revolve my body and resolve space. I might and she might, and I might forever and endorse that little-boy-first-touching-stance. Even as a man. Who am I, really, but up-thrust eroticized dust still testing the scrotum? Waiting, as it is, for the scandal of the painting in Paris to subside, for her to shave the color stubble and encourage me to taste, once and for all, the underarm scar? I wait for the moment and breadth of my breathing dispersed.

It Is Impossible
Not to Be Brutalized

There will always be departure, whether it be mud or blackbird dirt. If I am an actual revelation, then consecrate my mortal reply. There will always be a hooded brute. If I am the great nothing of the human egg, then distribute me as an indirect object in someone's diagram of the stars. I am immaculate in my shame. I have come to conceive the holy ladder between chakras. The single spinal nerve is an ascending angel. It is impossible not to be brutalized by human skin. What might it mean, where might my mouth, not to exert brute force? How might the moist of my ear inhabit your lamps left out, hobbled to the moon. *Yes, no, maybe. Sometime-after-eight.* Are you crying? Are you composed of dirt, of lost black birds? Are you crying?

The Sentence

for the poet, _____*

He lives, he said, for the pure joy of a sentence, for the
slantwise grip slicing back through the clock. Scissors
hands laid out on the table resemble a ballerina exhaust-
ed from the weight yet still pointing one foot forward
toward the food that could be and one backward toward
a thinning wire that passed through her cells and shaped
her. *Poets belong to a cut of the World,* he said, carving his
name in seven languages over and over in secret into his
chest. He knew the letters by heart. He knew the chest
hair would be years in growing back. He knew his hand
would sweat and tremble whenever he smelled lead and
heard the dog pant and express its stool. He knew the
heart would be near and far. He knew he had blood on
his hands. A Chinese junk slowly crept by from out of
the bathroom mirror into a burlap cloud, then into the
mouth of a frog, as if no longer needing water. The sail-
crumple, what he felt every time he collapsed a word and
unhurled it from his chest. *I keep thinking that if I could
write, I'd write not a Bible, not the Psalms, not the Koran nor
some Upanishad, not even warm peony blossoms of T'ang
Dynasty love, nor the pumping forth of bleached blood-angels*

---

* Reader insert one of the following:
a. name of poet believed to be subject
b. name of author of this prose poem
c. if different, name of *both* believed subject *and* believed
   author (otherwise repeat name)
d. reader's own name (if female, change pronouns and
   anatomical references accordingly)
e. name of favorite inanimate object with poetic propensity
f. none of the above

before me on the table in piles of speckled sea salt, nor weeks of split shifts without sleep, nor thin shaved legs afterward in the clutching in the dark, nor newly fallen snow without the salp or the seed, without spleen or wing. A quonset hut glowed in the snow-covered night, and so much substance piled around it at the roadside as if he might learn not to swerve, as if camping at midnight in the echoing slush of passing trucks might relocate a gravelly period between letters and not sentences, words. *We write,* he whispered into the bathroom mirror, *toward the excretion of the personality.* He wanted to write not a Bible, nor the Psalms, nor some undiscovered Upanishad, nor even a controversial verse for the Koran. He wanted breasts and he wanted milk. He wanted the red red snow of peony blossoms. And he wanted them now. He wanted the night-glow of the quonset hut as sun in his groin. He wanted a scrotum without motion, without pearls, though the pearls could come, he conceded, if that was the only way to finally find flight.

WANG WEI BOARD GAME

WANG WEI BOARD GAME

Begin with hexagonal-shaped flat playing surface (circular surface may be adequate substitute, but it loses the opportunity to resonate mathematically with the sixty-four I Ching hexagrams). Square boards are ill-advised, particularly during certain lunar phases (see Meng Chiao, "Fourth Discourse on the Four Corners of the Four Parallel Earths," 53).

~

One to six players may participate (adults, fourteen years of age or older), up to three "yin" players (females, eunuchs, or effeminate males) and up to three "yang" players (males, or mammals unusually fascinated with sun in their own groin).

~

Select board token as your principal participant "identity." Choose among the following, one for each player: wandering monk, Chinese timber wolf, panda chewing bamboo, lute, Mongolian pony, emperor's fingernail (pointed, curved token), Tu Fu's ragged overcoat (token with holes), amorous palace peacock, courtesan, Yangtze ferry boat (without ferryman), River Han ferry boat (with ferryman), panda without bamboo (sad-looking token), full moonlight (elongated, translucent piece), Tartar warrior, blood pheasant (red-tipped winged token), apricot grove moth, river wave Li Po drowned in (token marked luminous with dissolving star), Subprefect Chang (government official token), court poet, yarrow stalk, bamboo rain forest (large, slightly damp token), and conscription officer.

Play with same token for duration of the game. However, once a month, it is advisable to switch identities in order to understand logic of other players.

~

Begin playing at moment moth appears in fluttering moonlight at window sill. (Obviously, the playing of *Wang Wei Board Game* can normally only commence at night.) If no moth appears when all players (or self if playing alone) are (is) huddled around board, it is permissible to darken room, light candle, and wait. If after five minutes still no moth appears, game may commence if light rain begins falling upon magnolia blossoms, or at the moment mist descends. If seasonality does not permit blossoms and/or mist, a very light snow will do.

~

To determine order of players' moves, each participant must compose *shih* verse; finished poems should be judged (preferably) by wandering stranger, but if no stranger passes abode where game is being played and/or can be recruited to judge, children may be asked to rank quality of poems. In this latter case, under no circumstance should adult players offer children persimmon leaves or sweetmeats, for they may interfere with brain power and impair judgment of growing child.

~

First player rolls dice (preferably, use single die so as to avoid needlessly dichotomizing perception of cosmic experience). *Wang Wei Board Game,* when played on hexagonal board, ends at beginning and begins at end. When game is played in round, each player station should be duly bathed in moonlight. Die with single dot on all six sides is highly preferable (as per above), but 1–6 dots per side may also be used as long as no side contains same amount of dots (which would again diminish opportunity to dissolve dichotomous thinking). Second die may also be employed if players desire their token to advance around board more quickly (however, keep in mind that *Wang Wei Board Game* works best when forward motion is focused on less than actual experience of being part of the "larger game").

~

Round One:
Sample throw/move (first player): Player 1 (wandering monk, for example) rolls die (dice) and lands on third square, depicting portrait of jade equestrian vase. Draw corresponding card which reads, "You have been asked by a wandering stranger (seemingly senile) to play your lute for a handsome reward. You play beautifully, moving a crowd of onlookers to tears. When you finish playing, the stranger hands you a dead guinea fowl as your reward, asking if you agree that death is indeed 'handsome.'" You (select one of the following in order to determine further move): 1. kindly thank the stranger and continue advancing piece in proportion to 1/100th of the feathers on fowl; 2. humiliate stranger by degrading his dead ancestors, whose names you must first locate in the public record; 3. politely point out stranger's error, ask for thirteen gold pieces, and depart, advancing token thirteen spaces, careful not to allow token to wander into barbaric north country; 4. write a poem in *shih* verse on the spot and tape it to the stranger's back, blindfolding him, and prodding him through the street with a bullwhip while kicking dust onto his shoes.

Once player selects option, move token appropriately.

~

Sample throw/move (second player): Player 2 (lute, for example) rolls die (dice) and lands on fifth square, depicting T'ang Dynasty watchtower. Square reads,

"Take two steps backward and draw two cards." Third square's first card reads, "You have been asked to accompany Wang Wei on a visit to Chungnan foothills. Keeping in mind that Wang Wei is both a painter and a poet, which of the two (painting or poem) would you prefer he compose near banks of Yellow Flower River?" Given there are two cards to draw, Player 2 (lute) has option to answer or to draw next card, which (for example) reads, "You have gone with Wang Wei in search of Master Wu. After a vigorous mountain trek high into Chungnan mountains, you find that Master Wu is nowhere in the monastery to be found. Nor is he meditating quietly by nearby mountain stream in bamboo grove. A stranger approaches you and (although you are a lute) asks you to play the lute for a handsome reward." You (select one of the following in order to determine further move): 1. Play yourself beautifully, arguing that there is no authentic self outside your own textual strings; 2. ask the stranger first for a guinea fowl in whose stomach your strings are stored as freshly-eaten moth eggs; 3. ignore the stranger and request to be stroked by the beautiful hand of a lovely courtesan; 4. express sorrow that Master Wu will not see nor hear you play yourself that day.

Once player selects option, move token appropriately.

~

Interlude to Deal With Possible Superstition:
It is believed by some that playing *Wang Wei Board Game* can cause genital warts. However, there is no hard evidence to suggest that this superstition has any merit. If, on the other hand, burning and/or itching occur during play, it is advisable to seek medical attention immediately. In such cases, amorous palace peacock token will be selected to hold the place of the temporarily departed member. This token, it should be noted, is not a move-

able token. It must also be placed on the square acquired by that player's second to last throw/move. If that is a yin square, the amorous palace peacock must face south; if a yang square, face the peacock north. Play resumes when player returns and replaces peacock token with originally-chosen identity. He or she receives up to one extra throw/move.

~

Sample throw/move (third player): Player 3 (emperor's fingernail, for example) rolls die (dice) and lands on eighth square—*The Gate of Pleasant Dew* (cited in Buddhist Fa Hua Ching, and referring to the "entrance into nirvana")—depicting thick pine forest, winding river, and deer barking in the moonlight. Draw corresponding card which is blank. (Do not advance token but enjoy bathing in conscious moment of eternal infinite void, depicted by the number 8's symbol of infinity.)

~

All three players take brief interlude, join hands, and —although conjoined with consciousness of Wang Wei—conjure spirit of Li Ho. At this moment, Player 1 should find depiction of peacock embroidered on his chest. Player 2 should open shirt. If female, retire into adjoining room (with—preferably heterosexual—female hand servant) to witness the opening of the blouse. Once blouse is open, Player 2 (witnessed by hand servant) should find tattoo of 27 dead birds on breasts and arms, and (with arms raised) on freshly-shaved underarms, above calligraphy which reads, "Shamanic poet, dead by age 27, did not live as long as the great Master Wang Wei." Player 3 should refuse to open shirt (or blouse, if appropriate), while remaining players bet on possible depiction.

~

Round Two:

Sample throw/move (third player now goes first, in order to seek harmonious balance of eternal Tao): Player 3 (emperor's fingernail, for example) rolls die (dice) and lands on thirty-first square, depicting Mt. Shihlo in background of burial site of Yin Yao. Draw corresponding card which says, "Draw no further cards." Player is expected to compose a poem around the opening lines, "There is only the stream that flows / down to the world of me." Complete poem and place on depiction of stream (see either square 51 or 63). One is life stream and one is death stream, but which is which will remain unknown until end of game. Place poem on depiction of one stream or the other, and sprinkle water with sassafras root on poem until brush stroke of calligraphy dissolves, joining the "world of me" with the world of the eternal river of either life or death.

~

Emotional Interlude:

If life/death decision emotionally upsets Player 3, a brief pause (to regain composure) is allowable, but each player may only request one pause per game, with that pause resulting in the loss of next move.

~

Possible Disruption:

Stranger pounds on door, demanding admittance, saying he understands the group is playing The Game. If two-thirds of players agree, he may join but not as a legitimate player. However, the only piece that can be made available to him is Tu Fu's ragged overcoat (token with holes). (Thus, it is advisable for group members not to choose this piece while initially selecting tokens, in case of the unforeseen.) Stranger gets one throw/move only and can take it at any time during the game, even if it lasts for days. However, only yin squares are available for movement, and he may only use one die. If stranger's throw/move lands him on a yang square, he must recuse himself and supply the group with wine for the duration of play (Tu Fu's ragged overcoat token is then retired from this particular session). Important: under no circumstance may the stranger make eye contact with any already-participating player. If he does, he is immediately disqualified and may (under extreme circumstances) be banished for up to one month from the province.

~

Sample throw/move (second player, who—with three players—still goes second, even when reversing order of players in round two): Player 2 (lute, for example) rolls die (dice) and lands on square 3. Immediately proceed to square 6, then double each jump to 12, then 24, then 48, then circle back to beginning after reaching the end (board concludes at square 64). Since next called-for square would have been 96 (the doubling of 48), subtract 64 from 96 for appropriate square from "start" on which to begin again, and rest identity token (as described in the I Ching's 64th hexagram, *Wei Chi / Before Completion,* "every end contains a new beginning"). This would be square 32—*Cemetery of Dead Ancestors*—depicting piles of bones, human remains, cremation ash, and weeping woman slashing wrist with sharp stone. No corresponding card is given. Instead, player must contemplate whether he or she belongs on square of death. Rather than card, inscribed on depiction of bones is the phrase, "Yes you do. Now you, too, must weep." Player 2 has option of weeping or throwing die (dice) one more time. If weeping is chosen, player must sit at board, head bowed, and—rocking back and forth—cry for duration of game. If, on the other hand, throwing die (dice) is chosen, player moves accordingly.

~

Sample throw/move (first player now goes last, again in keeping with harmonious balance of the eternal Tao): Player 1 (wandering monk, for example) rolls die (dice) and lands on tenth square—*Hostile North Country*—which depicts barbaric Tartars copulating outdoors with multiple partners, living in yurts made of animal hides, engaging in Mongolian pony races, and eating dead raccoons skewered on knives. Draw corresponding card which reads, "You have wandered into the barbaric encampment of your own soul." You (select one of the following in order to determine further move): 1. ask barbarians philosophical question dealing with a certain thorny religious matter and the ethics of Confucianism; 2. attempt to convert the entire encampment to Buddhism; 3. discover that Tartars are so caught up in the Mongolian pony race that they believe you are another pony; 4. ask for directions to the mountain hermitage of Master Wu, several thousand *li* south, certain that—though you appear sincere—the Tartars will still execute you as a matter of tribal honor.

~

Rounds Three, Four, Five, Six, and So On:
The above samples of two complete rounds of *Wang Wei Board Game* should suffice for continuation of game. Play as many rounds as you wish, the key being to attain full cosmic consciousness while playing, with players completely merging their consciousness with that of The Game itself. Again, it is highly recommended that players change principal identities at least once a month, or until they have learned all they can regarding a particular principal identity.

Menstruating women are especially encouraged to shed former identity and select a new one each month to correspond with time of menses. If *Wang Wei Board Game* is played during period, it is best done 100–117 paces from menstrual hut of servants and (if played during days of heavier flow) will likely serve as mild advantage to women who embody universal flow described herewith and in the poems of Master Wang. (Menopausal and post-menopausal women may also enter the game with confidence, providing they sip cherry juice prior to each throw/move.) Although they may play with a somewhat heavier heart, menstruating women will also have the further advantage of understanding the joyful sorrow of Wang Wei's lilting lute through windless bamboo.

~

Concluding Advice:
Finally, it is advisable to be a practicing Buddhist, accomplished painter and/or poet, or skilled lute player when playing *Wang Wei Board Game,* or—at the very least—to become one of the preceding shortly after the game commences. If, on the other hand, a player is Confucian or Taoist, or even follows a Shamanic sect, it is advisable to participate in special Tu Fu, Li Po, or Li Ho editions, respectively, of *Wang Wei Board Game.*

Bee Entrails Alight
With Cosmic Fire

FROM
THE BOOK OF TONGUES (7)

I have been writing *The Book of Tongues* all my life.

At age three—even before I could write—my *Autobiography of a 1950s Greek Divorce* began, "And so I can no longer tell who loves whom, whose tongue is whose."

It has been written in *The Precision of the Acrobat* that at age five I could sit tongueless watching both *Rin Tin Tin* and *My Friend Flicka* simultaneously on the same t.v.

My *Book of Tongues* brought me (arguably early) hormone activity and Debbie Metcalf, who I asked when I was six whether her "things" had started to grow.

And so it is written that I was born tongue-tied, with two frenums. One tingling with the ectoplasm of every woman in the world. The other, a mime in the attitude of a cactus thorn. In *Autopsy of a Boy,* it is recorded that it was Dr. Ashwell who clipped the outer of the two. Which that was is said to be unknown.

"There was a death-knell in his knee that somehow surfaced in his ear."

All right. I admit that I did not write each and every volume of *The Book of Tongues.* There are many books in the series, as there are many tongues. Some were even written about me centuries ago by *rishis* in Himalayan caves.

One passage from *A History of Mirrors* foretells how in 1967 Jimi Hendrix would be a sparrow flying from my eleven-year-old chest, and how "this boy would, thusly, search for owl resin evermore."

It is even rumored that a secret Upanishad foretold that I would only find solace in Paramahansa Yogananda's *Autobiography of a Yogi*. But that, "after age sixteen there would still be many years and struggles of tongues to follow, as a holy means of clarifying butter."

Several volumes were never written, only spoken, with some only thought forward and back like a crosscut saw into willow wood and birch.

At nineteen I lost (admittedly late) my virginity to a woman named Margot, while making love completely naked but for a sagging left gray cotton sock. (There is no mention of this in any of the volumes of *The Book of Tongues*—written, spoken, *or* thought.)

Thus, it has been believed by some dying leaves that it was actually I—not John Bradley—who composed the seminal study, *Autobiography of the Prose Poem* (originally titled, *The Prose Poem as an Orgasmic Sock*).

It has been rumored too, but never confirmed, that the shameful texture of one of my luck-tongues co-authored both Eric Baus's *Dissection of a Prose Poem* and Ray Gonzalez's *The Prose Poem's Hidden Diphtheria*.

Once I read that I could never be the kind of friend for which I'd hoped, but it appeared in a series of clichés in an unauthorized volume of "my" (so-called) sad poems, *Magic Moments in the Sand Castle by the Sea*.

It is written that, "There was a hole in his heart where bees had forged a liquid ear," but exactly where is unclear.

In *An Extended History of Love,* one chapter describes my life with my wife as two bee entrails alight with cosmic fire, smeared across a Sophist cave wall.

Need I describe the importance of a core volume, *How to Treat Your Beagle as Your Only Child*?

Then there was the Vallejo tongue. The Hernández tongue. The Elytis, Ritsos, Seferis tongue of torn Aegean blue. Even George Harrison's ashes lapping the placid skin of the Ganges. Each a clabbering in my milk-deficient moan. All described in *Your Esophagus and You,* somehow, by certain cankered passages known only by the presence of salt.

For many years, I once heard, I even confused *Brahms* with *Brahman,* the oversoul of his lost baton.

I mistakenly killed an ant when I was six, and, henceforth, in precisely fifty-three volumes, its invisible tongue appears as an x ray of my own skeleton.

There is, finally, flaring pink folds in my chest repeatedly humming the closing lines of John Bradley's poem for Li Ho, "Brown spot on a pear, / Brown spot on a pear, / Who shall come / to woo you?"

I have been writing *The Book of Tongues* for as long as I can recall, even before my passing. From thought to tongue, tongue to thought. One life at a time.

BELGISCH CONGO,
CONGO BELGE

It's been thirty-nine years since I sailed the River Congo, northeast to a village in search of Kinshasha. It had all been simple pubescent pain. Hunched in a room thirty feet from the divorce, I poured over squares and rectangles of inky blue, slate, carmine, olive gray, listening to the bend of grass huts across river from the French in Brazzaville, hearing my mother and new father argue over drumming and dancing and pounding falls about the cost of lawn furniture, the merits of cold mashed potatoes, the young blonde flirt with long legs in the Wednesday night bowling league in Lowell. All that unresolved doubt she must have felt, and me, clinging to tall men haloed in ostrich feathers who pressed spears into the African veldt like fierce spines that stood me right in bamboo groves far from Indiana, where I was certain my light was destined to be darkly lit.

My father never phoned again when I slipped that first September and called my new dad, *Dad*. Nine years old was too young for a life sentence, I knew, though I had my own room, and black and white t.v., and got A's in Phonics and English and Math. Full-bellied zebras, round-rumped okapi, and undressed breasts fed into me from below. All I knew was that the stirring in my groin was the pound of pouring water I longed to touch, and in touching, clutched the desire for more. *New wallpaper,* my mother said, and the hall blossomed velvet roses raised slightly like gooseflesh a mid-August wind might suddenly bring in remembrance of books and bells. *Shag carpeting,* she spoke, and the den was drenched in orange and rust. Even the plastic rake hid in the closet, fearing the bend. As if reaching down that far might be enough to strain the prongs and make it break. An artificial palm, she stroked the brush of his five o'clock shadow, and the living room was almost alive.

Beyond the Port of Matadi, all the way past Leopoldville, hunched within the parameters of a perfect perforation of thirteen, was Inkissi Falls. I knew every hang of those falls, every leathery boa river bend, the River Ritshuru, the River Molindi, the Suza, even east of them, by land, through the bush and plane trees of Mitumba across the border to Ruanda and Urundi—occupied German East Africa. Spoils of war. I knew the bottom dropped out for a purpose. I knew the man with the wooden spear would splinter bamboo forests in rain and fight the Belgians and save the village from malaria, missions, sleeping sickness, and flies. Huts wretched in the wet. The smell of straw mixed with cow urine and dung. The salt and juice of life that shot out warm and thick and sticky and further than the Belgian nuns might go, or *could* go, that lent more, even, to the land than the argument over Christ or Thunder, Flemish or French.

More potatoes, my new dad would say, and the plates were filled with blots of boiled light. *More pot roast,* he'd request, and mother would brush the bend of red hair from her face and smile over the roaster as if this time she'd cooked it right. *More milk,* and she'd suddenly blush, forgetting, for a moment, the blonde and bowling and Wednesdays and legs. Congolese was what was really spoken, especially in the rain forests near the falls, but no one understood because they were too concerned with contemplating the merits of Flemish and French. *Belgisch Congo, Congo Belge,* I'd hear myself say softly over stamps, turning my head gently to the left three times like an exotic striped fish foraging silt. *Belgisch Congo, Congo Belge.* And the tribal crown of ostrich feathers. And zebras in foal. And full-bodied bosoms in carmine and slate. And blossoms dimmed by the night light in the hall coming velvet through cracked doors. And the touching beneath sheets for bamboo leaves or a spark. And spear splinters in the wet. And the unceasing equatorial heat.

LIVING IN THE MATERIAL WORLD

for George Harrison

How can I ever say your name, George, without bleed-
ing my own dark flower? Gentle rose gardener, in some
previous life you fashioned a term for the word *salt*.
Then, one by one, sparrow secretions from the sheets
returned to breath, and the axis of earth stopped.
Whether a word flexes color from the phlox matters
most and doesn't matter. At least, that's what the bush-
men of the Kalahari believe as they count the legs of
centipedes back to a blood ring in their right ear. You
knew that sound, George. Sang it sad. Strummed it
hopeful. Chanted it toward dissolve. One by one you
counted the people who counted their toes, confused,
when they heard—through bones of the head—crow
tracks in the dust. You who set the owl ablaze in my
chest, waking me with memory of what I might make
of the joyful sorrow of being alive. Incarnation after
incarnation of dust storms I'd once been, of paramecia
I grew from in the Gobi, from a goatskin scroll in a
Calcutta vase, to the magnificent spine of now. You
who navigated the narrow harness, the muscular pulse
of the arching neck of a dark horse rivering through
rapids of gossip and strain. Even the praise that prom-
ised to lock you into the slow spacious blood of expec-
tation, while the world was busy birthing an egg. We
loved the same lover, George. Our divine clutch com-
plete, again and again, as we cross ourselves sad from
river-mirror to river-mirror, from Sanskrit script
among the scrolls of the whirl and the slow blood of an
ear, burning up desirous seeds of living in the material
world while counting hairs along a centipede's back.
For the many legs of our lives matter most in the reach-
ing out from a center that centers us whole, dark horse

in the dark pulsing waves of a seed not unlike the bleeding from a hoof, not unlike the carbon of a bone-burning hide.

CHRISTMAS AND
THE BEADS OF SWEAT

for Laura Nyro (October 1947–April 1997)

You were never booed off stage, Laura. That whole
Monterey episode, an urban myth, or was it a miscue,
the *boo* you heard rather than the word, *beautiful?* I
always wanted to make love, make life with your voice.
To exchange secret fluids of bodily sound in the coupling
assonance of *Laura* and *George*. I don't think I ever heard
as much pain as the horse galloping through your dust,
across each track, that full-veined neck straining in your
soul as you sang "Been on a Train," "Talk to a Green
Tree," and, of course, "The Poverty Train."

No, you were
never booed. Monterey just wasn't ready for your New
York flash—that black gown and nails. Hair fixed back.
The smooth smoke gravel of your Gospel grit, fierce
like a caught carp among cats. I never heard such pain
but sensed weeping in the slow pools, in the fratch cap-
tured at your act. And one word. That tri-colored syl-
lable—*beautiful*—heard ever after slantwise through
your throat like drift-dungeon bones, or was it a mono-
chromatic *boo,* beautiful you?

So now it's April, and you're
dying all over again, all over *me* again. It's the furthest
sun from Christmas. Still the trembling exists. Light
falls dim upstairs from a Chinese lamp. Take my hand.
Touch my cheek. Your voice or mine? Succulent sweat
beads up on a plum we may or may not eat, that we
might hold between us, oddly large, like a moment of
indecision. Sweet sweet sweat, droplet upon droplet,
like a necklace of skulls around the neck of our cosmic

Mother. How you devoted your life to. How you became and kissed. How you bathed, tummy-touched, and grew.

And how you died that eighth day of the fourth month. Strange doubling of dates. Left at the end of your fourth decade, not quite your fifth. That phrase rolling around, twice as loud, without cracks, like an unspoken egg: *cancer, ovarian cancer.* Such an inverted birth.

I hear the smooth rough of your tongue, examine again that photo from your *Mother's Spiritual* album, admittedly still get aroused—a bit guiltily now that you're gone—by your downcast eye, your smoke tree hair, that full lip that appears to contain all the salt and sad. Wondering what the woman you touched touched in your cheek. You, piano woman pacing the keys. Pressing my need. The space you open this way, that. Gospel-crowned jewel, you were never booed, at least not by me. Nor by John Phillips, nor Lou Adler, nor that outspoken dude stunned by your voice as you finished "The Poverty Train," crying out *beautiful, beautiful* up at your stage.

But you always remembered that '67 California day. Jimi, Ravi, Janis and Big Brother, the Airplane, Pete Townsend smashing his guitar, even Brian Jones—fully caped—roving like royalty among the thanes. How you thought you'd dressed all wrong—your New York jazz and slip. Your east coast nails. Your nineteen-and-only-second-public-appearance. Your facing-a-crowd-and-about-to-be-alive. I've seen the footage. I've seen the slinky dress, the dramatic hair and hips, your back to the scene. I've seen you turn to sing, smog of rabbit trap in your eye, the shocked blood at the instant that word's cold teeth snapped metal and latched its *boo beautiful* jaws onto you like refrigerator burn to a plum.

Darling Laura, they never *booed* you—something, I hear, you could not accept. And you never heard your voice the way we did—how truly beautiful you were, how beautiful you are.

TONS OF SOBS

for Paul Kossoff

The sexual articulation of fruit. The erotic texture of
plants on the table. Salt passion. Cassava root. The
medicinal properties of oregano. Desire, like a mollusk,
to grow a palp. He looks up at the night tossed whole,
the knife naked from its nest. Enters the stars as any
spring dispersal, as would any soft crustacean. Checks
the ticking of his heart. Interrogates the beat of one two
three / one two three.

What cut holds his blood? Where might his mouth?
How come and for how long? There is no reason, he
realizes. Never any reason why the longspur has settled
its wing on his sill. Why the season of mangoes has
abruptly moved to an end. An houri inexplicably
arrives with her mouth-hungry breasts, wearing only a
huckabuck for a gray cotton slip. A yes-two-three / *yes*-
two-three he massages as her hip into the interior of his
ear. The scarred erotics of rock? The in-his-ear-but-not-
really-there? The how-long-and-for-how-many-more?
Where might his moist, his magnificent mouth?

And so, the tongue as an instrument of pain? Paul, why'd
they call you *Koss*? Didn't they realize that *Kos* is the sec-
ond largest island of the Greek Dodecanese, that its
proximity to Turkey makes it, in moonlight, always
about to kneel? Seems it was Segovia who must have
taught you best, who gave you—as you mimicked his
records—your first finger callus, your childhurt name.
Then, at sixteen, catching Clapton with John Mayall's
Bluesbreakers, sending you back to the guitar to form
your first band, Black Cat Bones. You who lived the
blues. Couldn't you recognize the way pain eventually

breaks, disperses as night peppering *your* bones, gives you a proper balance of fruit and spice, black and white? A ballast of music in your one two three / one-two-three chest? So why the white powder, the dead-at-twenty-five, the trademark vintage Gibson Les Paul left unstrung in a corner?

You had it, baby. Your fluid stew. Slow, melodic leads. Your gutsy bluesy riffs. The word *Free,* not just a concept but a fierce entwinement of tongues. A somehow-confined that called into question even the veracity of plants.

Paul, you backstreet crawler always about to birth a blues. When they took you off the plane in New York that March 19, it was coconut pulp, I hear, that they found for a heart. Your young-man's paps moist with a gently-threaded weeping of milk.

FROM
THE BOOK OF TONGUES (33)

dear *Book of Tongues,*

We are reconstituted regularly by what we discard. An orange crayon. Foreskin. Nail clippings in the sink. I have been born so many times I can no longer count. Which is one reason I am determined this time to stun myself out. Sun myself on some piceous rock and, at some Gobi noon, simply dissolve.

And now my enormous Russian expanse. That Doctor Zhivago train that keeps pulling me away from everything I love. The problem with most problems is that they encamp like Red armies and White. Sure, our blood is blue prior to the oxygen rich of tongue. Yes, our palms are lighter in color than our thigh. But a whirl of two's keeps us on this train. Which at times resembles eel sliver through fog. At others, an extended tongue, an ache oiling the nowhere track.

I know. I, too, have been mocked for my reliefs. Which is one reason I'm determined to sky. Not by groundswell nor belief. But through mapping my own cognition dissolved to sound.

You say that you wrote *me* into this enormous heat. That you were just minding your own business in some clay pot, in some shop corner, propped in some dusty West Bengali town. That a man and woman, soon to be divorced, in touching tongues from across the great ocean, imagined my any human pain. That seed became sound became strips of Greek descent screaming in December flesh on Chicago's South Side. But I never *wanted* to breathe, unless it was the underwater commotion of eels igniting one another's egg.

And now my exemplary egg. And see-sound stirrings in Aegean light. And this mouth with which I am hung. Well-so, like any Greek feat. They call me *George* to mock me. *Giorgos,* as if I could be complained. Containers of sound are all we are. You and me, dear *Tongues.* For the nerve ganglia in my medulla hold as much script as the letters of your lisp.

Which reminds me, how am I to address you—dear *Tongues*? dear *Book of Tongues*? dear *Faceless Grain of Salt*? Tell me, what am I to do with your dearly-most-deserved article? Place the *the* instead of an *a,* and constrain to you, dear *"The" Book of Tongues*?

You see, I am not above such rendering. Such lode-rope, such vowel. For me we are discarded regularly by what we crayon, or foreskin, or clip. In the sink, we bemoan the moaning of everything and most all. Of swirls of thought creaking their own level, as if the gravity in pants finally gave out and our tongues watered black the chalking. Like any human pain never wanting to breathe in or out.

So, Gobi my tongue toward dissolve. Doctor Zhivago my brain with piercing triadic screech and snow-driven steam. Ask me my blame. And never, never forget, dear *The,* dear *The Book,* from whence I came.

I Am a Thorn in My Mouth

I am one point in the transformation of a corpse.
—Yoshimasu Gōzō

There is a tiny Shetland pony on my tongue. On my tongue, an Old English sheepdog barks and barks, blinded by its own hair, lunging for fetlocks and hooves. There is an itch in my pants. In my pants, a tiny Shetland pony shakes loose his soul as a flowing yellow mane, shakes loose his stool as tight damp curls. A border collie circles the farm. Going is coming back. Tomorrow becomes a tub of clipped toenails. Even table salt knows the blurry boundaries of black snow as it tastes the asphalt loops below.

There is a tiny orange stitch on my tongue. On my tongue, a fish spine in a basting pan, embossed as sunset field skeletons longing for the sea. There is a stitch in my heart the size of pants, and no one knows how much water denim can actually hold before becoming silk. There is a stitch the temperature of planets as they approach the boiling point of human blood. As they lose a sphere and drift toward the mall. As they shop for Bierkenstocks and clogs. Yesterday was tomorrow. Yesterday is a toponym for *not here, not here.* And every silkworm in the world develops an aversion to home, to the salt and the match, to the fabric and the noose, the shirt and tree.

I am a thorn in my mouth, I hear myself say. Touching my chest, growing breasts, tugging for the milk. Tonguing for the sea. *I am a thorn in my mouth,* and even the canker sores score over with clots of cantaloupe. With methods and seeds. I find myself saying *No* almost always whenever I answer their threads. *Would you like to die tomor-*

row? No. Would you like to go bankrupt? No. Would you like to join the war? No. Would you like a toothache and a hangnail from precisely 10:05–11:53 every other Tuesday morning? No. Would you like to meet her and finally get the blowjob of all blowjobs?

There is a drop of milk on my tongue. On my tongue, a leopard's bladder is loose. It's been staring for hours at its still spots in the pond, sipping the Milky Way from dark green pods. There is a thug in my heart. And there is a thud like gravel sequestered in my stool. Bending over and looking becomes bending back and weeping. Drying one's tears becomes letting one's blood. Even the barometer on the barn door tells me Venus is near. Even the border collie lies down to sleep below my tongue with a great sigh. *I am a thorn in my mouth,* I hear myself say. I search the silk and am full and wanting and stiff. I loosen the secret patch of curls with perfect fingers, breath, and spit. I part the pony's mane and count the burrs as tiny buds of grief. I tongue the silk and hear cocoons scream inside the trapped white wings of cranes in her kimono. *Oh, I am a thorn in my mouth,* I tell her again and again in the slurred, almost-true language of juice. *I ache whenever I speak. I ache whenever I don't speak,* I massage into the joints of those cranes. *You're special,* she replies, breathless, rubbing my spine, and then dissolves in a dust-mote moment of midnight waffle dream like smoke through a screen. And, tugging and tugging, I crawl her name through the dark. *Come back,* I beg. *Not here, not here,* I almost hear her say in the far-off puffs of lightning bugs. And, tugging and tugging, I cannot call the milk.

FROM
THE BOOK OF TONGUES (22)

All night ( )
I swallowed (long) my ( ) tongue,
reaching up through my scrotum,

>   past the seeds

to confiscate a rib,

>   over
>   and (a)gain
>   until I:
>   a. came unskewed
>   b. ate myself (raw)
>   c. *ibid*
>   d. my *yes* inside my *no*
>   e. required the consistency of an opening
>   action verb

But something green died inside
at the lashing back of the summer
of some great northern tongue,
charring my name forever
as the swimmings of eels
into *The Book of Tongues*

the way swiss chard cooks (codices)
its celery seed self off
into a pot of not-yet-steam

>   Until
>   Marcel Duchamp walked by,
>   hand in hand with:
>   1. Max Ernst, minus the tea leaf
>   2. Meret Oppenheim, without her
>   most moist fur

3. Madonna
4. Madonna and child
5. a urinal of hope—if not *for* all the lost tongues, then for what they
6. rehearse during the re(solution) of "The Great Urethra Debates"
7. the electric hope of my scrotum— could be my tongue, could be Georgette Magritte's (in my mouth), could be the how and cry of my life's midd(l)e name

LIGHTNING

When the man emerged from the lightning strike, every-
thing was eerily calm. The sea gave back its coin to the
insomniac. The tortoise chased the squirrel and climbed
the oak. The Indian he saw on East Pontiac sipped bour-
bon from a plastic bag. When lightning emerged from
the root, everything gave light—strawberry blonde or
auburn braid. The quarter on the silver tray inside in the
dark, the unshaven hairs on the mother's left leg, the boy
touching himself in the pantry near the cookies, even the
ink pen spilling itself dry of parakeets. The mathematics
of the night slept coolly with tables of the moon, with
the hips of street lamps repeating themselves suggestive-
ly to the man's gloom, and he rose to find the noise that
was making no sound. He rose to find the noise that was
making his mouth. Dry, he rose to find forsythia brim-
ming with tiny yellow stars. To find his own reflection
from the dirty window spilled back as a gold carp. He
had already lived forty-eight years and still felt fin-flash
as fur? When the root emerged from earth, the world
seemed to stop. A clump, a worm frozen in a dirty bou-
quet. Syllabic spar of iron combs keeping the tongue.
The Arabian's tail lifted in perfect bloom. Coins of the
aspen no longer roiled with sleepless salt-water slosh.
The Indian no longer debated the merits of Fort Wayne
over Santa Fe, no longer drove himself mad with a false
arm and bag in which he kept Korea contained in a diner
napkin in torn Chinese calligraphy that spelled *soot,* that
sounded like *ash.* The squirrel crept into the bird's wing,
slept in its sing-song noise. Calm. Everything was
almost, nearly perfectly calm. Even the hips that con-
tained the pantry-spill of flour. Even the man emerging
from the lightning strike walking away from him—what

gave light to the quarter, the cookies, the street lamps
bending suggestively with every curve—the lightning
sway that swelled his hair.

IN DISTANT LANDS

Of the inner life of the Japanese the world at large knows but little. One of Veretsc Hagin's paintings has made us familiar with this place, where the devout Hebrew seeks his Wailing Wall and mourns, in open air. The Japanese have a saying, "See Niko before you utter the word 'Splendid.'" A race of Gods or Giants must have inhabited Baalbek many a century ago. The head is said to be of gold bronze. Its nose is nearly four feet long. Little prayers are written on small pieces of paper and glued on some of the images, not chewed up and spit at them as is the custom in Japan. The history of the opium habit is humiliating to all who value humanity or honor. Opium was first smuggled into China; it was recognized as an evil as early as 1729. This tomb can be compared only with the Taj Mahal. The umbrella-shaped dome is said to be of solid gold. Covering twenty acres, perhaps more. This mausoleum is one of the finest and costliest tributes ever paid to a woman. There is also the legend that St. Christopher carried the infant Christ across the river somewhere in this vicinity. He will be left upon his knees, framed to a board behind him. Through this board a hole will receive his pig-tail queue, his toes will be tied to the frame, his feet left dangling, his hands caught back and both thumbs tied to the frame. Wings attached to his feet, the caduceus in his hand. It is a strange incongruous set of images, before which to burn incense and offer devout worship. Policemen enter with the biting bamboo knout. Some are sad, some merry, some are in tattered garments and bare feet. Many carry away bottles of water to be used in baptism in distant lands.

IF

If the moon suddenly broke water in your left eardrum, would it feel like a halo widening into a sphere of Saturn, bending your head, your entire weighty sunflower, to the left? If the men come and give you a casket, place you in it face down in paisley tie, will you regard the silk from your past differently, that black stocking of your wife more like dusk or a hurricane approaching you from below? Do you wish for it over and over until the olive tree itself splinters and walks down to the river and Miguel Hernández is there waiting for you with the affectionate knives? Do you lean against the dishwasher and fantasize about a tomcat humping cabbage leaves just before it dies from the concussion thud of a sparrow that suddenly collapses against its head? Do you tap your skull at midnight and hear the bones of your face strain to expand rigid fingers? A drop of leopard milk oozing from the tip of your penis? The moon in the throat of an owl ruffle and lift toward something hollow? The day may be calm, the afternoon fierce, the evening quiet. If afternoon starlight spun invisible and crackled like fire, would you ask the neighbor girl at the lemonade stand for a nickel? A toy truck? A pink plastic jump rope to tie your hands together at your groin in prayer? The guy down the block selling Bibles for a piece of leather on which to bite? A prayer card with a blond Jesus and the loving memory date on which you were born and on which you first tasted the forgery of a fig? When you pull the earth apart to plant iris bulbs, what is that purple burning the bend at the back of your throat? What bird sings in the Chinese elm with your vocal cords and the step of your weight that leaves traces of threatening sky on pointed leaves?

BONE-WORSHIP

Hey John,

I just found a stack of unanswered letters in my desk tray and apologize for having been too swamped with work the past few months to offer a proper response. Figured I'd jot answers/replies to some issues you brought up, and I hope you have copies of the original letters you sent, as this is the easiest way for me to catch up. Thanks, & much love—George

~

How neat. I never would have thought of inserting a pomegranate seed there!

~

Yes, I miss her too. And when you see her next, give her a big hug from me.

~

I prefer the earlier version of the poem you sent, especially the final stanza. Here, though, I think I might still suggest some minor revision. Have you thought of inverting the closing two lines so that the tiger is actually embedded *in* the bear? You say, *surround a mouth / with sound,* but I wonder whether the word *tongue* might be inserted, at least inside the bear's ear? For it's here where the *bee* and *sparrow* already reside, at least if I'm understanding the earlier reference to Elizabeth Hurley and Cindy Crawford. I'm also not that fond of your seeming overuse of the indefinite article in the closing, but mostly in the penultimate stanza. The indefiniteness of meaning disturbs me, the lack of a clear referent being unsettling.

~

Wow—no, I've not seen that film, but it sounds great. I love Indonesian art and Malaysian food and Bengali music and, even, sea salt on my mashed potatoes.

~

She's fine. Spunky as ever. Sleeps at my feet while I write, though she's out back right now hunting for cats. Speaking of which, I hope Luna's over the trauma by now of your new morning diet of pickled herring!

~

That's a tough one, buddy. I would think, yes, you might be able to receive permission from *someone* for that, but to actually *exhume* Vallejo's body might prove more difficult. Please don't let my sense of this deter you, however, because I think a skull-decorating tribute is, in many ways, in keeping with his wishes, as subtly described in his now infamous *Autopsy on Surrealism.*

~

Nope. Can't say as I have.

~

It was Takiguchi Shūzō, not Nishiwaki Junzaburō. Although I've seen it described in *Poems of Dadaist Shinkichi* as well. In any event, I'd say *morning glories.* Could also be *sparrow secretions on the sheets.* And, no, I'm not bothered by your use of the color blue, or even substituting it for *a bleed of green* (though I wish you'd quit bringing that up).

~

Yes, absolutely!

~

63

I can see you haven't yet given up on the idea of draping marigolds around the skull and skeletal shoulders of our beloved César. Okay. Here's some context for my response to this when you first brought it up a half dozen years ago. In India, I've seen linga and yoni (symbols for the phallus and vulva) similarly revered. But they are mostly made of stone, and the mineral deficiency is rarely (if ever) felt by the *entire* crowd of onlookers, whether or not they have accepted the trance. I *do* think there's a case to be made for sympathetic nervous response (and, frankly, I'm not wild about your implication here about what I may or may not have said to Simone). And, yes, I think your sense of widening the sphere of pain is imperative, but I'm not sure I feel qualified to make the call that you have an "inherent *right*" to eavesdrop on the dreams of perfect strangers, especially after inviting them to a seeming tribute. Perhaps consult with Vallejo's widow? Probe his shadow with a stick? Throw the I Ching? Circumambulate a nest of cold cobra eggs? Or, try sleeping with a copy of the *Autopsy* under your pillow to see what seizes you.

~

Really? A *pear* skin?

~

Ah, not too bad. But sometimes not. At least not in any given autumn.

~

Well, you know beagles. It's all nose. And I wonder, sometimes, just what of the world I bring back to her each day when she sniffs my pants, and what she *sees*— just by virtue of licking my hand.

~

She said *that*? About *me*? Well, don't give her a hug for me next time then! At least not when you're aroused.

~

How neat. I never would have thought of using nose-hair clippers for *that*! Don't worry, amigo, I won't mention it to *anyone*. You've got my word. But why not disguise it and use it in a poem sometime, transforming it into some other metaphor for intimacy and betrayal?

~

Oh, in about another two weeks or so. Maybe sooner.

~

Yes, of course I'll call first. And, yes, the tomatoes have been incredible this season. And, oh, yes—again—on the idea of Ernst-like (opium green) moth wings and camel-hair mustache. I do think it's important that our mothers both learn how we construct our voice in relation to our childhood and teen years. And I realize that confiding to them the weight of the calluses is important. But I'm also not that comfortable bringing up the idea of a third skin.

~

Thank *you*, buddy. I wouldn't have thought of it without the wind chimes you sent me years ago. Not to mention the tuning fork, which—I admit—did take me aback a bit when it first arrived. But no, I've never been big on herring.

~

I think it's called *Dream Caused by the Flight of a Bee Around a Pomegranate, a Second Before Waking Up*. 1944, I believe. When Dalí still really had it right (and long before those unsettling Alka-Seltzer commercials of his!). But, it also might have more to do with Takiguchi's Surrealist attempt to harness sound *as a form of frightened soup*. Oranges? Okay, but probably only in the event that the pears have shrunk. Anyway, hope that helps, but *be careful*.

~

Try Vallejo's widow, then, or the French Consulate (remember, he died in Paris). Forget the llamas. And, as César himself once said, *fuck the condors*. Keep me posted. I'll be especially curious about the size and texture of the marigolds.

~

A bit like Jim and Ray, perhaps, but maybe more like Phil. Though it's all a bit cloudy to me right now. (I notice, once again in the new poem, the lack of definite articles and absence of a clear referent. Is this a new series? How am I to understand this lack of context? What gives the meaning *meaning*? What do you hope to say in the gaps between images, even from phrase to phrase with such vast juxtaposition?)

~

Well, the most recent was a dream about you and me and a wooly mammoth (which had moments before been a heron). I was on a road not unlike those in Colorado, near the base of Sleeping Elephant Mountain. I stood not ten feet from the mammoth. When it suddenly reared and roared, its enormous tusks seemed to glow. I was in awe, completely without fear, until it eventually lumbered away down an old logging road, the armor of its hide dry and more rhinoceros-like, as if plates of the earth shifted across its back with each heavy step it took further into the wilderness. (I remember thinking of those elephants in Kenya doing the "bone-worship," knowing their dead ancestors just by the scent of a discarded tusk, licking the vast skull, passing the bone through the herd, trunk by trunk. How the whole elephant was available to them, even when it wasn't.) Then somehow you and I were together near evening, drinking tea, and you had to know every last detail of the sighting and where I actually saw the mammoth go. To respond to the rest of your query—no, I have not been dreaming of Vallejo the past few weeks, but I did scent marigolds once upon waking. Even *felt an exuberant political need to love*. What have you been up to?

~

Sure, but what time?

~

Probably.

~

Not sure I can, but I'll sure try. What shall I tell her about your tongue? She's sure to know it's mine. Especially when she holds the pomegranate and dreams of each of the rings of Saturn going blood orange.

THE PREPARATION
OF BONE GLUE

Even the Java Sparrows
Call Your Hair

with feet of Java sparrows drinking
—André Breton

And so even the Java sparrows call your hair *sand,* call it *seed.* And so even the shouldered tongue tones the lice. Lice of flower, lice of squid, lice of the torn kite tail your breath remembers but cannot swallow when it inhales nine times again beneath that star over you when you were nine. Quick star, dead star. No, nine stars spurring your chest, still, like tentacles, confused heads of sunflowers sinking for moons. Island home of fire, of the fourteenth rib, of the drone string of the sitar constantly calling from your own bone. As if a ghost tail is not, could never be, enough. Such a stop. Such a sparrow. Such a green cup you hold and sink from and want to hide inside. *Celadon,* you hear yourself almost blink, as if it were your shame. And with each sip, she, woman of the pale green invisible string, tongues your pen with the tame blood of a dead parakeet, with the celestial flood of many sting-beats. Six. Your blood was six when you mistakenly opened the cage, exhaled into late-afternoon leaves an oak in the missing bird that became your life. No, that had *partially* become your life until you found a now toward sound. A sparrow like the clarity of a broad-shouldered man housing beeweave as mound in the tube hidden in his limp on a rainy street. Slick street, dead street. Left street glistening bear hair hum across which you scratch your name as you talk. And if the wood should burn, the talon grip of the sitar might bleed the street, stir mud in the bottomed cup, might singe the rail yard that refuses to couple train to track, the pain's lack that lies always in the distance like sickness or health, or some tongue or other searching for bed in the beloved haze of 3:13 a.m., in the cup of warm milk at 4:37 and its lightning splash of dawn. Scent of cinnamon and vanilla and all that it could sleep. *If* it could sleep. And if an egret rises from that groinal dust, a sparrow foot might scrawl your flour so loud it becomes your lost and future bone. Clear bone, ninth bone. Bone of the fourteenth sting, with and without sleet. Bone of ground red cloud, of the snapped tentacle of swarmed lice that surrounds moon with moving light that bathes the tongue's afternoon rain, dark Indiana oak pain that makes your prayer an urgent yet crass reciting of calm. In the tail's slash of wind. In the kite's call (and all that childhurt grip can kill). In the continuous crawl of hair. That is and is not what grows into, what eats away from, *sand, sound,* or *seed.*

A HISTORY OF SLEEP

Animal skins from the time of Eden. Hunters with boils, appearing from Emmaus, believing in inverted stars. Eating locusts. A nipping in your half-sleep when you turn over the day's plague as hair crowding the pillow.

~

You found the earthworm and left the clods moiling in the moonlight. What could not be put into love? Pried into an earwig? What cracked like a word broken across the black bread?

~

Someone said, *A sheet draped over the leech.* Another, *Give me a fries and a Coke.* The stirring in your groin. Heat as she reached for the cup and revealed secret hair stubble.

~

Like lice picked from the hide of a cow. Your left shoe somehow larger than the right.

~

We were inmates of the dark kitchen. Given crusts. Told never to believe a lay person nor a monk. The window, the size of those in Flemish paintings. The cup of boiled milk had a skin of cinnamon, was smaller and larger than your only mother.

THE PREPARATION OF BONE GLUE

I am walking the night streets of Paris, completely naked except for a pair of gray Ragg wool socks and two giant moth wings growing out of my back. They are the black velvet green of a 1920s opium couch and open and close when moonlight surfaces and submerges back into a bank of clouds. Black antennae bend like dark wands in wind. There is not a star in the sky, only Venus, and I have the desire to look over my left shoulder and say the name of my mother three times softly like throwing salt on a path of fallen red maple leaves. *Georgina,* I say. *Geor-gina,* I repeat more slowly, tonguing the night air with the exaggerated thrashing of a gold carp at the edge of a temple pool. *Georgina,* I clench once more with the strain in my turned neck and rush of blood from the bend. From behind me, a man with a leg cramp walks past, sclaffing the ground with his left foot as if tapping for water. He doesn't notice me but several yards ahead suddenly turns and calls me by name. *George Kalamaras. You're that vegetarian from Indiana.* I'm startled. *How do you know?* I ask. *It's the moth wings,* he says. *You've taken such good care of my moth wings.*

He looks like somebody's bald uncle, ready to play roulette on a Friday night in 1920s Paris. He has the crush of a rain-moistened cigar. He resembles a peregrine falcon, his nose hooking into river fog wafting up from the street. *But I don't know you,* I think, afraid to hurt his feelings. Who is this man with the limp of a bird dragging a broken wing? *Yes you do,* he suddenly hears my thoughts. He peels off his falcon head and is a lion, mane matted with Kalahari sand. He peels off his lion head and is a Victorian woman, face controlled and withdrawn and gorgeous like marble above her tucks. He cracks the marble and is an owl, then a falcon again. He rips tufts of fur and is somebody's bald uncle. *I'm Max Ernst,* he says. *You just don't remember because you haven't yet been born.*

I run to embrace him. It is so good to see Max Ernst again. My eyes well with river mist but suddenly begin to burn as tiny street pebbles and flecks of sand ease out of my tear ducts. He hugs me, gently tapping my moth wings, stroking them like two lost and returning dogs. *There, there,* he says. *Green,* he says. *Solidified light from fading gas lamps,* he says. *The twin swans of Breton,* he says. *A pair of beautiful opiated broccoli heads,* he says. *Mirrored spots on a tissue of René Daumal's tuberculous phlegm,* he says. I want to take them off, give him something real, something solid, tell him it's okay. That they were never really lost. That like anything truly loved, they're his, even if for awhile they weren't. That like gray-green morning glories they just close sometimes when the moon goes cold behind cigar-fate clouds. That, like jaundiced skin, they sometimes shrivel to protect faint inner layers of dermic light, the velvet flight of birds at dawn leaving a field as sudden shotgun fire, sparrows returning all at once to a telegraph pole at dusk. *We must prepare the glue,* he says. *Wrap the tubes from your bones to narrow your blood,* he says. *Sap the marrow into a laboratory glass through a rubber hose,* he says. *Place the coils directly on your skin,* he says. *The hot metal plate over your groin,* he says. *Lay you on the couch and coax starlight into your ears so you can hear the deaf man's symphony,* he says. *Stroke those wands and brush your wings to stimulate the juices and the pulp,* he says.

We walk hand in hand looking for a place to lie down to hook up the hoses and tubes and plates and to prepare the bone glue. I am still naked, and a drop of sperm oozes from the tip of my penis, onto my left sock. It is warm and sticky, a drop that becomes a tiny puddle, then a small milky pool on top of my foot. I think of René Daumal coughing phlegm in lotus posture in India at dusk. It stays there on my sock, collecting dust, insects, a bumblebee, a torn pink tissue. It is so wonderful to see Max Ernst again, after all this time, and after never having yet met. I inquire about my mother. *Is she a lion?* I ask. *An owl? A peregrine falcon?* And he tells me she will be a cloud, then a shadow cutting water out of a red cobblestone pebble in Zurich, then a grain of sand from the Kalahari, then a red ant in the Gobi, then a morning glory seed so blue it will have to be born in Chicago, where I will follow, screaming for breath on the South Side at precisely 6:18 p.m. on a Monday on a December 3 not too far from now. *The night air will be cold,* he says. *But you will be warm,* he says. *Inside where the omphalos blood will bathe your wings,* he says. *And your wands,* he says. *Which will be my wings and wands,* he says. *Which will open and close, close and open as your mother breathes you into each turn,* he says. *Which will then massage her vagina when you are born,* he says. *And ease her pain,* he says.

I am so happy, holding Max Ernst's hand, moved to tears, because I love my mother. Love the memory of the scent of her red maple leaf thighs. Love the taste of salt when I turn in any grocer's to touch a tomato and recall the steam of her spaghetti sauce bathing my face when I would hunch into her pan. Love these wings now that I understand the shyness beneath gas lamps of the color green, the first light at dawn easing out of the throat of a freshly dead sparrow, of a fallen spear of asparagus before the coming of the killing frost. Love the gold gasp of a carp as it thrashes against a green marble floor, veins of stone familiarly cool like fresh fish blood but air oddly oxidized like sipping through gills a lock of burning hair. I am so happy, walking down the street with Max Ernst, hand in hand, because I love my mother. And because I love Max Ernst.

The Light Those at Work See

In the meeting room, a man pulls on a tie. They pass
around a peapod on which he signs, in paisley script, his
middle name. A woman he has admired for months lifts
her skirt just above her left knee. She purses her lips
slightly and reads someone's annual report in the ultravi-
olet rays of an iris. Zebra fish pass through the sound of
silver in her voice. Her ankle shivers, a little, beneath silk
with the memory of ice water on a June night and a bell
at her waist. Inside the peapod, a man pulls on a tie.

~

At the truck stop, a man removes his sweater and puts
on a coat. A plate of grits tightens as it prepares itself for
the anger in his stomach, for the thread of silk coiled in
his large intestine. For the miles in his mouth, dust from
Venus swirls in blue diner light. Collard greens, like
exotic fever, crawl from the kitchen. A feral dog sudden-
ly remembers the night soil around a certain cactus. Nine
miles away in Geronimo, New Mexico, the bone in his
neck begins to throb. A man in a truck lights a cigarette,
puffs perfect smoke rings, and sees in the passing lights
of cars the slant of Saturn.

~

Outside the convention hall, a drunken man takes off his
pants, rips tufts of hair from the left side of his head, and
points to the emerging moon. Flies gather at his groin to
sift the dampness of corduroy in the burgundy dusk.
Inside, a sinking yellow light edges into the blackness of
a woman's straps. She feels the tug of silk at her shoul-
ders as her breasts expand, slightly, from the salad she
had at lunch. The men in the boardroom are not her

mother. They are dressed in suits and have the heads of lions. They want mayonnaise on their ham, they want their rolls hard. She leaves the meeting, steps outside onto a crack in the sidewalk, and lifts her skirt. Two hummingbirds emerge like bats from a cave. It is evening, the sun is a red vine, and they are hungry. Dust particles from Venus almost come together. They go to work on the falling light like an incarnation not yet born.

TEASER

for Tommy Bolin

Because you are the cartographer of bones. Because the lisle thread of your lip. Because the sweet burgundy got you hard. And all the lost tribes of callus and sweat. The hidden salt of the family, the campanulate lisp that, as a child, forced you to sip cambric tea. Hot water, milk, sugar, and such a small amount of leaves. What more could one hope for from the childbell of hurt to the rock-circuit threshing for grain?

Tommy, you teased us with a life too short. You blew in at seventeen with Zephyr and blew out eight years later through the tubes in your own amp. Marshall Stacks and something like smack, where the amplifier glowed you to a slow burn. A strickle of sound leveling off your life at the rim of a tin. Cup. Saucer. Needle and spoon. Foundry tool used to shape a mold in dust-mote mounds. Saturn turn of the great wheel burned, burning, burnt. How to conjugate heat? Denver, Miami, West Berlin. Tell me, can we live by guttural elongation simultaneously in more than one place at a time rather than in the fixed shame of our name?

And why *Tommy* rather than *Tom*? I consider *Tom* McGrath. *Tom* Fool. Even *Tom* and Jerry. Each with a life thousands of mounds longer than yours. What if instead they'd called you *hyssop,* or *Eurasia,* or *Paleolithic pain,* or *recreant recovery*? What if your first solo album, *Teaser,* hadn't "teased," if *Private Eyes* wasn't so "reclusive"? And so now I think of *César*—Chavez, Vallejo, even Cedeño— and want to boycott grapes and conduct a thirty-six-day fast, write Surrealist poetry and die in Paris, throw a runner out, say, at second from a near-double to center.

Tommy, you've been dead twenty-eight years and only lived twenty-five. Your name keeps Saturn-turning you young forever, and your flaming riffs whiff through me surgically with the synergy of a young buck's cape. Because you are the cartographer of stones, charting a rich mineral rinse, a path of cold inert stars. Because the bones of your hand snap and mask a sleep. Because the lisle thread and the lisp. The undergarment and the swage. Long-haired heart misplaced in the chest of 70s tracks, you grew in campestral fields, came to Boulder, Colorado a camel and returned us our tongues, offering our dryness a camellia and stitchwort tea. Star-shaped flower acting like a weed, teasing us white in jazz-blossom garden grunts with the entire place of your name. Teasing us, Tommy, with the long season of a love lived large, timbre of a time too breathed.

CIPOLLINA'S RAVEN

on the fourteenth anniversary of the death of John Cipollina
(August 24, 1943–May 29, 1989)

Sallow-grained tremors in a dark dissolve. A brook of ecclesiastical bones. What is the weight of your dead right hand as you float your guitar-self, motionless, above the bed? Smoke-stained strain, smoke of your sad. Did you feel the rabbit-snap of emphysema trap and shock your blood into the inevitable stare? Hear starlings from the next county over banquet their beaks into your trembling chest? Beautiful gunslinger, after George Harrison and Jimi you were my favorite. Your sitar-sound rib dissolving my ground as if every note you played you played through water. Chronic current of what's dead to you concocts the hosta's heavy bow in rain, bend of pranic seeds we'll all one day breathe. Monastic mane of hair, cut uneven down your back. You, on stage with Quicksilver Messenger Service at Monterey, at The Fillmore, even when I saw you with the Dinosaurs at Denver's Rainbow. Toting your six-string chamberless heart, you played Russian roulette on each smoke-filled stage.

Where have you traveled, traveling bodiless now as you do? Is it true a bruised peony refuses Caspian moon? That in the other world walruses' mating habits describe the *yes* and *no* of cognition, that forced at the rim we scent the Arctic Sea in an air hole is nothing less than terribly cold? That the Arctic Circle is not actually drawn but inscribed on a line of mind into ourselves as pain? That your strange greening of bones, moss-pocked with age, is a gratitude to two packs of Luckies, each day your holding out for sound dissolve? Gorgeous electric guitarslinger who wore California, why'd you summon

Cipollina's raven so soon? Why'd you store a strobe permanently in my chest so all light long I hear the growl on "The Fool," question the "Pride of Man," and hear nothing but "Mona" moan?

Now the light of your lost fourteen years retraces itself back into the dead waves of the Caspian, into the hobbled sunburn of a blind raven in the Punjab, retracting back to Isfahan, into the Gobi stones you spoke. Slender holder of sitar-shade tremulous in a guitar growl. You understand the epidermal patch, the copperhead that bit you, how you continued to smoke even with the oxygen mask. Your siblings Mario and Antonia, in an Italian café, extinguish the hope that this year you would have turned sixty. You understand the path of bones, the luck of the draw, John, that even here, far from the Bay in an Indiana woods, the color green defines itself by how many trees one can distinguish from the stand. A book of blood? A brook of *yes* and *no,* of *this* and *that,* keeps collapsing like a river or a lung into itself, splaying your name.

ONE OF ONLY TWO

for Rory Gallagher

I was saying your name, saying your name backwards
that day. Like a contour map of your brain. It kept com-
ing out *monastic transplant on a hill.* Then, *fourteenth
Irish rib.* Then, *peaceful pineal acrimony.* Then, *where are
you? where are your shoes?* You gifted me a riff about a
"Laundromat." About some woman swallowed in tat-
toos. Bee entrails as a form of flight? The ink blue blood
of squids as what's strong in my vein? I'd thought you
alive, secreting my salt, till Ray told me—your liver
bloated from pink to black to gold, like a carp dying then
recanting the bruise. Strange draggling release of one's
color into the luminous texture of the next life. Rory,
you played the blues as if they were inked indelibly into
your skin.

Actually, into the liver. Compound, ventricular, versicle
gland acting in the formation of blood. One of only two
human organs with the capacity to self-regenerate.
Beneath your red flannel plaid something was sallow, as if
all the ink of your world squid-pressed into your shy and
your almost, into the well-depths of your smoke-throttled
voice.

It lodged there, spilling dark pearls backwards, each after
the other, that shook like fierce maraca seeds against the
gourd, that said *extreme nutation* and *one way, do not enter*
and *ask my name backwards but do the asking gently and in
one of three separate voices.*

From the alphabet, rare chemical dust. Interplanetary.
Diurnal. As if the left foot of the goddess Kālī firmed
your chest and retracted from your duodenum each of

84

the fifty-one letters of Sanskrit script into the garland of letters hung as skulls around her neck. I heard you wail with Taste on the Isle of Wight recording, stalk across the coals, blind yourself in each blurring seed. From within each sound, I heard the world dissolve. From *peaceful pineal gland,* I touched a little ground. From *as though a dreaming electricity,* your habile view.

There's beauty, Rory, in the amber lamp, the one you leaned against and held as you steadied yourself for the bed. The thrips at the bottom of your gut release strange thriving sounds we all know, but never speak, like tribal dust dialects of Upper Mongolia, untranslatable. Like keeping the night in a bosk. Like shad scum from that gland, we've all camped in a thanage on the heath plain of your brain.

You did me right since I was sixteen. Did us all consistent with your plight, as if you'd paddled yourself from Ballyshannon County, Donegal, up the Mississippi with a bullfrog in your pocket and let it swallow insects along the way, stinging the blues. I was saying your name today, saying it backwards. It came out *Irish fly swat.* Then, *Delta sunset hue.* Then, *pineal gland of crudely-bottled pain.* Then, *where are you? where are your shoes?*

GRIPPED BY AN UNDERTOW

for Randy California

How come you died in Hawaii, Randy, rather than
California? Off the coast of Molokai, mimosas blossom
a tare the weight of your hand. Same hand that shook
that of Hendrix, that in Greenwich Village in the sum-
mer of '66 as a member of his pre-Experience Blue
Flames earned you—at fifteen—the nickname from Jimi,
California. And it stuck, Randy, like meat to a wolf's rib.
Like spirit to flesh. Which is what you were before—
Randy Wolfe, born February 20, 1951. How come you
bled at the end only sea lice and salt? Left your guitar on
fire in beach sand? Bowed deeply, just before swimming,
before a nest of cold tortoise eggs?

Your not-quite-forty-six-tear-old body becoming beard-
years at sea. You walked the plank without even a plank.
Kapt. Kopter, what *were* the *Twelve Dreams of Dr.
Sardonicus?* Your breath now commands the fishes to
knock at your skull and eat the tender meat of your
brain.

But you knew this all along, didn't you, Randy
California? How you formed Spirit in '67, in spiritless
L.A., knowing that was precisely what it was all about.
That the body is nothing less than a gag. To keep the
mouth shut. To stunt the ears with beeweave as smog.
To hobble the tongue, in torn rope and bells, from
knowing the score of who and what we really are. At
night, on Sunset, you'd strut your wolf-bitten self at the
Whiskey A-Go-Go, at the Heat, maxing your axe across
the Strip from wolf howl to vowel. From pursuing the
purest mice of arctic ribgrass to the lice of living that
infested your chest.

And so your not-quite. Your blossom a tare. Your forty-five or -six. Your terrible body. Your becoming of years and sea, eased out as griseous bloat. Your most beautiful salt salting the world as layer upon layer of sea-sound or snow. Somehow before you died, you managed to save your twelve-year-old son, Quinn. Somehow you knew that your wolf-bitten hand had already chewed too much of the moon.

I've seen you circle the nest, claw the dirt through a cat's paw or dog's, lay down your body with a sigh.

A Theory of I as Inscribed
In an Examination of Me

a. I have been thinking again about I (me) and what
    I (myself) entail if entailment is even possible
    at this stage of evolution

b. It was in the tree, it was of the tree, and
    it *was* the tree   there was not any dying
    like breathing   hibiscus leaves blowing in wind

c. Christ and Krishna have the same
    etymological root, the same tuft of sound

d. Uncomfortable with the shift of text, he (she) adopt-
    ed second person (hereafter referred to as "you") for
    everything as one (perhaps two?) way(s) to grasp the
    ontological certainty of dust his (your) vacuuming
    mouth might stir

e. How might what we know know what we might
    become? If knowing is the possibility of

f. Migratory finches and aboriginal bees

g. Juan Ramón Jiménez wrote:

> *I am not I.*
> *I am this one*
> *walking beside me whom I do not see.*

There is gusto in Castilian control.
Juan Ramón also wrote:

Oh, where is Federico?
Oh, where is Miguel?
Oh, where is my divine hairy rat and my sacral
little onion head?

No—I (me) (you) wrote these second four lines
each night, stacking spears of asparagus crosswise
on a mushy plate of lemon and oregano beneath a damp
shade, contemplating a frayed green house
of elongated cards, of phallic vowels

h. She was said
    to have a heavy hand.
    She was:

    1. the new cleaning lady
    2. a prostitute with a metal elbow straw
    3. a woman with extraordinarily long arms
       who received speeding tickets in two adja-
       cent towns in rural Ohio
    4. an irritable mother scolding the kitchen sink,
       rubbing Comet cleanser into one half of a
       seared chicken breast
    5. none of these

i. This train might be home for the dead if
    not for chestnuts brought out of the fire

    south of Bombay at the Indian hill station
    south of Bombay at the Indian hill station

j. That dream of being back in Spanish class, being called
    on while working on trigonometry, asked to conjugate
    the trajectory of tick-tack-toe   the present subjunctive of
    your (its) (my) past   a gorilla, noticed only by you,
    walking in late, making coffee
    with a Mr. Coffee at the back of the room

89

B.C. The most sacred Indian art has a dimension of
guided eros

k. The first letter of everyone in the world's last name

l. You (I) were (was) born December 3 and hereafter
have always seen 12:03 inscribed in the clock-glow of
the universe   in the digital blood near the bed   as
moments to eat when the waiting list is full   as the hotel
door you (I) are (am) assigned on the nonsmoking
floor   as regulatory codes on those gas trucks I (you)
keep seeing on the interstate   as their Tibetan tantric red
hibiscus flame of approval   the effort it takes to
sip your name backwards through a   straw

m. Chocolate, chocolate, chocolate

m. Chocolate, chocolate, chocolate

n.

o. *Anything for a rupee,* pointed the twin rails toward
Bombay

p. You step from the Albert Street bed & breakfast, take
the bus to London Bridge, towards Big Ben. Feel
that freckle on your wrist widen, supplies of first aid
blood calling you as bandages from the banks. Did
you change (linebreak) dollars to rupees to pounds?
Who determined that exactly thirty-one rupees equals
a dollar? Or $1.56 for each British pound? Who
decided upon the transfusion of clocks for blood?

q. Juan Ramón Jiménez also wrote?:

Uh oh, I almost forgot Vicente.
His (my) (our) mother would never speak to me again!

r. True, false, or indifferent?:

   $$+ \; = \; -$$

s. You understand your weight loss not as the low fat
    diet of three months in India, but as a slipping off of
    something you never quite grew, that you could not
    sustain. Like that enormous tree from the center of
    your chest? Spinach and turmeric without cheese?
    Roasted *brinjohl* and *subszis*? Entire weeks in search
    of a spoon of peanut butter?

t. True, false, or indifferent?:

    2 plus 2 is sometimes just a cigar
    two + two = (occasionally) a cigar (chew)

u. Uncomfortable with the shift of text, he (she)
    adopted second person (hereafter referred to as
    "you") for everything as one (perhaps two?) way(s)
    to grasp the ontological certainty of dust his (your)
    vacuuming mouth might stir

v. Sunrays through the screened porch
    might make melanoma (melanin? melanism? mela*nite*?),
    might make you (linebreak)
    sick. (Better "you" than "me,"
    that is, if *one* believes in word magic?)

w. You step out of the gauze of an enormous clock
    in the mirror, say, *Oh my (I)!* Say, *Hey,*
    where's the (you)? Say, *December may not be the cruelest*
    month, but it's certainly the bloodiest. Witness: *the birth*
    bag burst, the twelfth month, the third day, the end
    of starlight as we (you, pl.) know it, as one

long chew the intimate vowel, a way of holding you
(me) back from vibratory fields of sound.

A sadhu with a trident on the banks of the holy Ganges

x. True, false, or indifferent?:

$$x + x = y \quad y + y = y$$

y. True, false, or an irritable chicken?:

$$y + y = x \quad x + x = x$$

z. *Let's start again,* she told you (me)
in the chromosomal (cloying?) kiss,
but you (I) were (was) busy with the gorilla,
with "new math," with the salp,
with conjugating Castilian (linebreak)
roses, and did not respond   your (my) (I) tongue
did not respond

A Theory of Zero as Inscribed in
The Book of Origins

A Sanskrit scholar stays the day studying the origin of the word *origin*. The point of intersection of coordinate axes is a Cartesian possibility that does not acknowledge the etymology of silence in a Himalayan cave, the syllabic pause of a *rishi* who ascends the spinal axis in *samādhi*.

He closes his book and centuries of soot disperse a cloudy aura around leather binding. He closes his eyes and accidentally discovers the secret mantras to be chanted at each chakra in the spine. He considers astrology, recalls the Book of Bhrigu, understands that seventeen stars tonight over the Bay of Bengal are the scars he will receive on his arm in sixteen months when a pan of boiling water will unexpectedly spill and make him want to die.

He cringes with the thought of such heat, tries to shake it off, remembers being fifteen and dreaming of fourteen forest eunuchs who came in the dark to remove his penis, cutting a flap of skin for a vagina. How they arranged thirteen mangoes afterwards on a brass plate beneath an altar of palms. How the mangoes pulsed, orange sea urchins tossed plump onto the beach, testing air like the deep sigh of a dog just before sleep, expanding, contracting, as they breathed themselves almost round, surrounding the curve of their own death, imagining mouths. How when he was twelve he fantasized about being rich, buying a hotel one day on the seacoast in Bombay off Marine Drive, having eleven wives and ten sons. Nine times a night he'd make love, and two of his wives would sleep alone with nothing but eight fingers and two sandalwood blossoms to tell his name inside them through the dark. How at seven he learned to write that name in cursive in six different languages. How the bones in his back snapped when he studied math, whenever he'd write his least favorite number 5. He had been four and unable to speak, but he could divide. And his three brothers had tortured him with the number *2: salt and pepper,* they'd repeat; *yes and no,* they'd smoke with adult-looking cigarettes; *good and evil, this and that,* they'd poke with their hands; *mother loves you, no she doesn't,* they'd touch themselves in private; *manly man and chicken shit; boy girl girl boy; heaven and hell.*

How one sight of zero was all he ever wanted, all he searched for in the calm of a mango, almost round but oblong from months on the tree. One hanging sight of zero was all. Even if it meant sleeping with his head polar south, coaxing the magnetic fields of a penguin to rearrange his photons as it slid head-first thousands of miles south down a snow bank into an air hole of freeze. Even if it meant the Himalayas were north and he might never sight the elusive Kashmir stag. Even if it meant he wanted to die in the shape of sound he might hear if a yogi suddenly tapped him on the chest and drew his breath out of the alternating currents, the inhalation of *yes,* the exfoliation of *no.* The possibility of exhaling intersecting sounds was why he sought the emptiness in zero, that pause in the hummingbird's flight, eating book bindings each night as strips of water-buffalo jerky, drinking kerosene without cause, studying the origin of the word *origin.* In name and without name. In book and without book. In fruit and without bough. In spine and without scar. In the starlit carcass of a camel. In the darkness of a Himalayan cave that snowed inside him brilliant whenever he didn't write his name in one of two languages, in the knife and chant of a forest eunuch, in the garden skin of four mangoes ripening, five of which grew in the attitude and jungle and wife-mouthed plough of unresolved sound.

Selfish[1] girl,[2] grow up[3]
to[4] be a[5] woman,[6] selfish[7]
tongue[8] in my[9] mouth
alone[10]
and—of[11] course—[12] full[13]
of[14] fright.[15]

---

[1] Once, about 8:30, the exact moment of 8:30 experienced purposeful isolation.

[2] There wasn't just Barbie but also GI Joe.

[3] Unica Zurn's anigrams, not to mention one drop of echinacea in a glass.

[4] The two turbaned men below have not been identified.

[5] the

[6] One less rib means one's skeleton rotting more quickly among the tall, lush grasses of southern July.

[7] A butterfly [Middle English *butterflie,* from Old English *buttor-fleoge : buter(e),* BUTTER + FLY, perhaps from the belief that butterflies steal milk and butter.] breathed through my skin.

[8] One plus one always keeps searching for zero.

[9] Butterfly fish, *Chaetodon capistratus.*

[10] She or he did not recognize him or herself while plucking an eyebrow in the mirror [nosography, nosology].

[11] Later, at approximately 12:03, I sensed my heart skip twelve, then three, beats.

[12] or

[13] Unica Zurn did indeed leap from a [fifth] second story window to her death. Her lover, Hans Bellmer, continued exhibiting dismembered dolls. A tongue free of coordinating, even subordinating, conjunctions.

[14] and; while; because; so; but; when; after; where; yet; before; or

[15] A butterfly breathed through her skin, was her skin [washer skin] and the winged rough of my tongue. Became my tongue. Because my tongue [became].

RECENTLY, IT HAS COME
TO OUR ATTENTION

that John Bradley's Takahashi Shinkichi book is said to be missing. Of course, this information comes from John Bradley himself, known—upon occasion—to fabricate even the shadings of food coloring of the beef stew. In order to determine the plausibility of his story, we ask that you consider the following and choose the correct answer. There is only *one* right answer, and—indeed—there *is* a right answer. Disregard of instructions indicates lack of Surrealist skills and will yield zero points, which may or may not affect your total SSS (standardized Surrealist score).*

John Bradley's copy of Takahashi Shinkichi's *Triumph of the Sparrow:*

a. was not lost but was either never written or it vaporized shortly after having never been written

b. was really stolen one night in Bowling Green, Ohio in 1988 by (a visiting) George Kalamaras as a Surrealist joke

c. never really existed in John's house in the first place

---

* This test is freely given as a service of the Institute for the Study of Poetic Sanity. Any proceeds garnered from taking the test, or any expansion of consciousness that studying the question might yield, are the sole property of ISPS, protected under development 28.5, section 3. Inquiries regarding the use of any change in consciousness, as well as rights of refusal (regarding poetic sanity), may be sent directly to the offices of ISPS, P.O. Box 1203, Fort Wayne, Indiana 46807.

d. was actually written by the dissolving sound of a spider unweaving a web

e. can be read in its entirety on page thirteen of the facsimile of Vallejo's *Trilce*

f. elongates the Bible and is, therefore, under house arrest

g. never really stored its melancholy self in John's house in the first place, though he formerly lived on Merry Avenue in Ohio and now resides on Normal Road in Illinois

h. is not equal to one fish or even a sparrow, but to two starlings fiercing it out in the chest of a disgruntled Buddhist monk

i. suffered a nervous breakdown and is, therefore, not available for comment—not unlike Takahashi himself in 1928 upon first receiving Zen training and who, sent home, spent the next three years locked in a tiny room

j. none of the above

FROM
THE BOOK OF TONGUES (35)

dear primordial joy,

I have been chewing on a bay leaf my entire vowel. Each elongated sound, a bee entrail enveloping my mouth. Tell me, can an elopement become sure as? Can it wedded to and entirely? Can it, like water, seek its own gravel? For something is rough and loose in my level chest beneath the tire spill of syllabic spit, and I am something if not nothing again and a bled and again.

~

dear there have been many,

Which means the months have piled since I last wrote you, seeking a richening of starsift in my left ear. There have been so often and awful that I don't know what to. If not *how* nor *think*, then at least three moths me in my mouth right now.

~

my dearest something less or more,

Summer rain. No umbrella. Frog swallowing scum of the pond.

~

dear Bactrian border,

Okay. I admit that I have been thirsty for far too long. Have enlaced this *Book of Tongues* with water and my most intimate. That I search for fluid in this speck of word. That I milk the sand that feeds me. That I lead a course of water but can't make it sink. Into my words spills part me, part you. And I am breaking apart like a long-inhabited ear, a star seed-sounding itself toward dissolve. Muscular mouth and membranous stitch. Which is what I hope for and expect, lying, as I do, upon this syllabic hammock of mold. Menhir. Long stone. *Magino.* Esophageal swathing of sound. Green is my back, and green the root. Green the spark in my mouth.

~

dear almost there,

There are six chakras, six churches, six candles in the spine. The swallow swims through fluid sky, swallowing hard air as if fishing far for a self turned inside out. A word seeking chert, sinking among the hidden fasts of the secret families. And a sky and a swift. My entire mouth I've struggled with it, even from the time I was six or had hives. To touch a poison planted below the tongue in a mother's childhurt look. To fend your life blaming your bay leaf word. Father this, divorce that. Thirty-six me with years spent in an anguished absence of fatherly touch. Anxious ears. Tasted tongue. Under the bed, below my saliva spill. Dirty talk in the mirror of a teenage mind absent of song or sung. For there are seven chakras, with one hovering above the head. By some counts, fourteen. When the spine goes completely and fully. And finally. And the entire egg of it lights up with words crossing the fault line of Mother *this*, divorce *that*. Of thirty-six years spent in ancient anxious clutch. Of *me me me, you you you.*

~

dear like a life,

Which means winter steam. The pony's mouth. Hoar-

100

frost on the hocks. Your secret self dispersed in cloud-kill from the belly of the world.

~

dear okay, you've got me,

Why do you swallow me from town to town? I am no longer breathing with anger. Seething from chert to chert. I am no one if not everything. Blue light hovering above the head. Seven books of Eden. Seven brothers of the well. Seven days of desert from Emmaus, from my meek and my might. Seven times two shades of Krishna-blue, of strings of sitar qualming the spine with sound in the midst of dearest-most-deserved depth. My *dear okay, you've got me,* which means, simply, two adults who could not get along and placed you in a. Which is when the tearing apart and the mind. Which is how the mud bath lathed. Eight maids a milking. Seven swans scrim-ming. And the sixth goose with one more or less tongue than a bull and a cow corralling the calm of precisely seven phrases of the inner and outer endocrine:

Eden / my entire mouth / thirty-six me with years

spent in an anguished / my entire vowel / seeking

a richening of / scum of the pond / sounding,

seed-sounding myself toward dissolve

101

Looking for My Grandfather
with Odysseas Elytis

I'm walking through the narrow lanes of Athens and Elytis is at my side, his right arm looped through my left. His bald head involved in some secret triangulated message-sending with the full moon and sunken sun. We are searching for the grandfather I grew up with, George Avgerinos, though he has been dead twenty-six years. *Not here, not here,* Elytis says, gently patting my hand, when I lean into a corner, when I crane my neck into the retsina scent of a taverna, salivate on the street near a woman in black and the open spit for a lamb, remembering my Nono, my brother Perry, and me dividing the tongue into three even parts. And though I don't believe him, I know he must be right.

Then we're in Zakynthos, the island of my grandfather's birth. "The Poet's Island" Dionysius Solomos made famous in 1822 and that now forever holds his name. Somehow we've left Athens and have crossed the Ionian. Moonlight resembles an asphalt bridge, lava floes of solidified sulfur at Minerva Terrace in Yellowstone. I look back and watch them dissolve in lapping caps and leaping hagfish. A Greek Orthodox priest emerges from a glass coffin. He has seaweed on his slippers. He wears a tiny gold cap, I sense that he is bald. He's Saint Dan, greeting us in demotic, saying something about *hair shirts* and *stones in the mouth at Mount Athos* and *retsina wind carving cliffs* and *lamb's tongue tucked safely in the chest of every newborn foal.* His censor floats through Elytis, and Elytis's cigarette suddenly catches moon-flint and lights. *Not here,* he coughs, that hearty, tuberculous cough of the many-smoked, thick clouds soaking us both, the lava floes reemerging then disappearing within the rasping strokes of the hagfish.

We thank Saint Dan, kneel and kiss his feet. I hear something about *my son* and *good boy* and *mind that tongue in your own chest now too.* Somehow both he and Elytis know my secret. That solstice night in Colorado nineteen years ago when I kissed the back cover photo of Elytis from *Maria Nephele* before writing poetry, before logging the first vowel. And then before sleep, kissing it again, slipping it beneath my pillow, holding my right index finger over the outline of his mouth as I curled into the darkness. *Drops of light, drops of light,* I had silently chanted, echoing Elytis's core, into moon-folds of sleep, into the sunken yet persistent sun. And now both Saint Dan and Elytis look at me, each clasping two hands together in air as makeshift pillows and, standing, rest their heads upon them, saying in chorus, *Drops of light, Giorgos. Vowel without end, Giorgos. Tongue in the chest.*

Saint Dan returns to his coffin, caressing the hasp, seaweed stains on the stones. Elytis takes me deeper into the island to a small village, a two-room hut. My great-grandmother, Angeline, is on the floor, the midwife spreading olive oil on her crotch. Pans of boiled water. The lantern carving out notches on the wall. *Here, Odysseas?* I ask, self-conscious that I've called him by his first name. First the kiss, now nineteen years later assuming the liberty of his Christian name? He pats my hand, saying only my name in Greek, *Giorgos.* I remember the gamey taste of tongue, eating it with my grandfather, asking why it was I who got his name. My great-grandmother moans, moon-flint again catching Elytis's cigarette. Something like a lava floe stains the birthing rug. It is beautiful and terrible. My great-grandmother's face tightened as in orgasm or broken bones. I want to cry out, save her, but I have no voice. Each time I go to speak, the ash on Elytis's cigarette glows more brightly, and something in my chest elongates through waves of saliva, crushing my heart, caressing my esophagus, flaring pinkish folds against my lungs. The midwife is now a giant fish, black shawl clasping the damp. Fierce gills pumping night wind, forcing some rasp in the shape of, *Push, push!* Elytis holds my hand, measures his breath to mine. He gently undoes my trousers, the buttons of my shirt, dabs sweat from my brow, rubs olive oil on my groin, in slow circles at the sensitive tip of my penis, on my chest just above the nipples where the crushing begins. *Push, push,* he says. *Vowel without end in the chest,* he says. *Soon you will speak, Giorgos. Soon you will speak.*

NOTES

Translations of the epigraphs are by the following: Rick M. Newton (Yannis Ritsos); Naoshi Koriyama and Edward Lueders (Kasuya Eiichi); Richard Arno, Brenda Barrows, and Takako Lento (Yoshimasu Gōzō); and Jean-Pierre Cauvin and Mary Ann Caws (André Breton).

"From the Book of Tongues (–13)" was conceived as my part of an ongoing correspondence with Eric Baus. Many thanks to Eric for his inspiration, dialogue, and cross-pollination.

"Soma: It Is Raining" was written after Stratis Haviaras, in honor of his "Soma" poems.

"I Might and She Might" is based on Paul Delvaux's painting, *The Visit*.

"Wang Wei Board Game" includes a quote from the I Ching, "every end contains a new beginning." *The I Ching or Book of Changes*. Trans. Richard Wilhelm and Cary F. Baynes. Bollingen Ser. 19. Princeton: Princeton University Press, 1967.

"From the Book of Tongues (7)" attributes a few lines about Li Ho to John Bradley that John has indeed written.

The poems "Living in the Material World," "Christmas and the Beads of Sweat," "Tons of Sobs," "Teaser," and "Cipollina's Raven" take their titles from album titles by the musicians to whom these poems are dedicated. Paul Kossoff, Tommy Bolin, John Cipollina, and Randy California were guitar players for the bands Free, Zephyr, Quicksilver Messenger Service, and Spirit, respectively, and Rory Gallagher, also a guitar player, fronted a band bearing his name.

In "In Distant Lands" the lines are borrowed at random from *Art Photographs of the World and the Columbian Exposition,* an album of rare photographs of the *Wonders of the Universe,* "Prepared under the supervision of the Famous Lecturer, and Prince of Travelers, H.H. Ragan, with accurate, instructive and entertaining descriptions by Emma C. Bush," Chicago: Star Publishing Company, 1894.

"If" was written after Sesshu Foster. Its phrase, "Miguel Hernández is there waiting for you with the affectionate knives," is a reference to, and adaptation of, Hernández's line "looking at knives with affection" from his poem, "I Have Plenty of Heart." *The Selected Poems of Miguel Hernández and Blas De Otero.* Trans. of poem, Robert Bly. Eds. Timothy Baland and Hardie St. Martin. Boston: Beacon Press, 1970.

"Bone-Worship" is dedicated to John Bradley and includes part of two lines of César Vallejo's, "[For several days I have] felt an exuberant political need to love" and "fuck the condors," from *The Complete Posthumous Poetry.* Trans. Clayton Eshleman and José Rubia Barcia. Berkeley: University of California Press, 1980.

"The Preparation of Bone Glue" was written after Edward Hirsch and takes its title from a painting by Max Ernst.

"A Theory of I as Inscribed in an Examination of Me" includes a few lines from Juan Ramón Jiménez, "I am not I. / I am this one / walking beside me whom I do not see," from his poem "I Am Not I." *Selected Poetry of Lorca and Jiménez.* Trans. Robert Bly. Boston: Beacon Press, 1973.

"From the Book of Tongues (26)" is for Delia Tramontina, who helped remind me of the mysterious muscularity of the footnote.

ACKNOWLEDGMENTS, CONT'D: The author thanks the editors of the following magazines in which some of these prose poems, or their previous versions, first appeared or are scheduled to appear: "The Sanctity," *American Literary Review;* "Tons of Sobs," *Arpeggio;* "In the Café of Strange Skin," *Barrow Street;* "I Might and She Might" and "Lightning," *The Bitter Oleander;* "From the Book of Tongues (-13)" and "It Is Impossible Not to Be Brutalized," *Conduit;* "Your Insides Have Some Explaining to Do" and "Living in the Material World," *Double Room;* "Even the Java Sparrows Call Your Hair," *Facture;* "A History of Sleep," *Flying Island;* "One of Only Two," *Gargoyle;* "A Theory of I as Inscribed in an Examination of Me," *Hambone;* "I Am a Thorn in My Mouth," "If," and "The Light Those at Work See," *key satch(el);* "Williams in the Hospital, 1952," "The Egg," "Teaser," "Cipollina's Raven," "Gripped by an Undertow," and "Looking for My Grandfather With Odysseas Elytis," *Luna;* "Brahms and the Taxidermies of Sleep" and "Belgisch Congo, Congo Belge," *No Boundaries: Prose Poems by 24 American Poets* (Tupelo Press); "The Preparation of Bone Glue," *The Prose Poem;* "The Sentence," *Quarterly West;* "So You Do," *South Dakota Review;* "Wang Wei Board Game" and "In Distant Lands," *Spoon River Poetry Review;* "Soma: It Is Raining," *Sub Rosa;* "A Theory of Zero as Inscribed in the Book of Origins," *Untitled: A Magazine of Prose Poetry;* "From the Book of Tongues (35)," *Ur-Vox;* "From the Book of Tongues (3)," *Yen Agat* (Thailand). The author also thanks the following for including some of the preceding in their pages: "Brahms and the Taxidermies of Sleep," *Arpeggio;* "The Preparation of Bone Glue," *The Best of the Prose Poem* (published jointly by Providence College & White Pine Press); "Looking for My Grandfather With Odysseas Elytis," *The Drunken Boat* (as part of an online chapbook, *The Transformation of Salt*); "The Sentence," *No Boundaries: Prose Poems by 24 American Poets* (Tupelo Press). The author also thanks Leaping Mountain Press for publishing a chapbook, *Heart Without End,* in which "Soma: It Is Raining" was first reprinted.